Women on the Way

Kevin Scully is the author of a range of dramatic and prose works. A book of meditations, *Sensing The Passion*, was published by Triangle Books in 1997. Ten of his stage works have been produced and two radio plays broadcast. An Anglican priest, he is based in the parish of St Dunstan, Stepney, in the East End of London. He is also Director of Ordinands and Vocations Advisor to the Bishop for Stepney.

Women on the Way

KEVIN SCULLY

TRIANGLE

First published in Great Britain in 1998
Triangle
SPCK
Holy Trinity Church
Marylebone Road
London NW1 4DU

All quotations of scripture are from the
New Revised Standard Version of the Bible © 1989.

British Library Cataloguing-in-Publication Data

A catalogue record for this book
is available from the British Library.

ISBN 0–281–05162–3

Typeset by Pioneer Associates, Perthshire
Printed in Great Britain by
Caledonian International Ltd, Glasgow

Contents

Contents

For Norma and Ken,
whose life and teaching
got me started on the way

Introduction

We are about to set out on a journey. We are about to follow the steps of Jesus Christ on his walk to death on Calvary. This has been done before, by particular people at a particular time. It was done by those who were there. Real people saw Jesus condemned to death. Real people flogged him and abused him. Real people sympathized with his plight. Real people spoke with him and heard him speak. Real people saw him die.

Yet for us, at a remove of almost two millennia, there is distance. We do not have some sort of time machine to go back to the days of the Roman occupation of Jerusalem. We cannot even use what have become the basic tools of modern visual communication. There is no news footage of the trial or what followed it. We cannot look at videos or snapshots of people who happened to be there. There are no newspapers on file from that time.

In many ways, we are forced back onto our own resources. What we can do, as Christians and others have done over the centuries, is to use our minds. In meditation and by the use of our imagination we can place ourselves among those who saw Jesus on the way to Golgotha. Again, these techniques are neither new nor original, but they can provide us with a potent springboard from which to make the impact of the passion real.

To help us do this we have some valuable equipment at our disposal. In the first place, we have the Scriptures. Each of the gospel accounts of the final hours of the Christ, of his passion, tells us a story. But we must not fool ourselves that they recount exactly the same story. Nor should we assume that every detail is captured within them. What we have in general is this: Jesus meets some friends in a house where a woman washes his feet; he goes to Jerusalem; he eats the passover meal with his disciples; he goes to the garden of Gethsemane to pray; he is betrayed, arrested, undergoes various trials and indignities; he is given the cross, which he carries to Golgotha where he is crucified and dies.

The gospels do not all tell the story of the passion the same way. Sometimes the events can seem dramatically different. Details recorded in one account may be totally absent from another. Things do not necessarily occur in the same order with the same people. The writers of the gospels wrote for different target audiences. The precise nature of these issues is beyond the scope of this book. What is of overriding importance to us is this: the writers of the gospels had a singular goal. They were united in their purpose. They wanted people to know something about Jesus.

Meditating on Scripture is an ancient custom. It was particularly fostered in monasteries. Its several techniques, known by various names, have a simple goal. It is to project oneself into the writings. This gets us nearer to the events recorded in Scripture. It is a method that can make us one of a range of people. We can be a spectator at any of the incidents in the final hours of Jesus. We can watch a woman wash his feet. We can hear him condemned to death. We can witness his nailing to the cross.

The same meditative process can make us come even closer than that. We can use it to become an actor in the drama. We may be a shouting citizen, yelling down Pontius Pilate when he suggests releasing Jesus. We can, if we are bold enough, imagine ourselves as a soldier who scourges Jesus. We might put ourselves in the place of Simon of Cyrene. We can allow ourselves to bear the weight of the cross of the Christ. We can hold the hammer that drives the nails into his hands. We need not fear we are doing the Scriptures a disservice in this. Again, the way has been trod before us. We have been helped by many artists. Paintings of incidents from the passion hang in nearly every major art gallery in the world. Think of the myriad paintings of the crucifixion. Poetry and fiction have taken their source from gospel accounts. The visual and verbal artists, however, do not confine themselves to a hidebound rendering of the events. They bring their own creative talents to the task. They use their gifts to allow us to see something new.

Imagination need not be restricted solely to scriptural sources. We have other equipment to use. Many stories have accrued over the passage of time that have their root in the person of Jesus. A particular insight can pierce the accumulated detritus of church conservatism. Fundamentalism has always been an anathema to real adventure in prayer. It continues to be so today.

Many myths and cults have grown out of the passion. Some of them are bizarre. Drawing on but one example, there is the cult surrounding relics of the 'true' cross. As has been pointed out on many occasions, if all the pieces alleged to be from the cross were gathered together, the Black Forest could be extended by its current acreage.

But extra-biblical sources have provided a number of enduring practices. First and foremost are the stations of the cross. Many churches display examples of these. Christians around the world make the prayerful progression of the fourteen stations throughout the year but with particular emphasis in Lent and Holy Week. They follow Jesus in body and mind as he moves from his condemnation to death by Pilate, through his struggles with the cross, his falls, to his crucifixion, death and laying in the tomb.

The stations of the cross are thought to have originated in the Holy Land, where Christians would stop and ponder the events of the passion of the Christ. The number of 'stops' may have ranged from anything between five and thirty. The practice of formal tableaux depicting certain events from the last hours of Jesus is reputed to have been started by the Franciscans when they had the custody of shrines in the Holy Land. Many pilgrims wanted to repeat these practices at home.

In the eighteenth century the number of stations was set at fourteen. These contain eight events captured in Scripture: Jesus being condemned to death, his taking up of the cross, the assistance rendered by Simon of Cyrene, Jesus meeting the women of Jerusalem, the stripping of his clothes, his death, his body being taken down from the cross, then its being laid in the tomb. Five came from popular tradition but we do not know precisely how they came about. They are the falls of Jesus, captured in three separate stations, his meeting his mother and his encounter with a woman known as Veronica. This latter encounter is a potent one. It is the subject of a chapter in this book. There is one borderline case, and that is the nailing of Jesus to the cross. There are biblical accounts of Jesus being crucified; there is no mention of nails until the post-resurrection appearance to Thomas.

Many modern sets of stations include a fifteenth, the resurrection. This is a salutary reminder that there is a resolution to and relief from the pain and suffering of the passion. It is the glory of the resurrection. Including such a station reminds us of the victory over death. We look forward to it and we glory in it. Despite this knowledge, we can put it to one side to allow ourselves a deeper experiential reflection on the passion. Such a disconnection is essential for imaginative prayer such as the stations of the cross.

The stations are a codified meditation. Progress through them follows a set pattern. The observance can be done alone or corporately. They can be followed silently or with formal prayers. Yet even the stations are subject to ongoing pressure for change. In some instances their number has been expanded again to take in incidents mentioned in Scripture. Mention of this will be made later in the chapter on the mother of Jesus. Suffice it to say that a number of pious traditions surrounding the passion of the Christ have been enshrined in the stations of the cross. While we may not know their exact source, they have been used to great effect in prayer and meditation over the years. They can still be of use today.

We may not be a Rembrandt or a Milton but we too have imaginative gifts. We too can use Scripture, works of art and pious traditions to see something unique in the passion. That relies on a simple fact: each of us is unique. What we experience is our own. Looking at a painting, reading a poem, meditating on a passage of Scripture or a mythical event can produce similar experiences in different people. But they are similar; they are not the same.

This book sets out to view the passion of Jesus Christ in a special way. It will attempt to set you on the way of the cross through the contacts Jesus had with women. This, again, is simply a springboard. Through those initial contacts we will consider other encounters Jesus had, with women and men, adults and children, before and after his death. Hence the title of this book, *Women on the Way*.

We will consider the women of the passion. We will be following women who met and talked with Jesus on the way of the cross. Our initial task is to concentrate on their experiences. This is not to belittle the passion. Nor is it to distract our attention from Jesus. It is not a diversion from the possibly distressing events of his final hours. Far from it. It recognizes a simple profundity. We must approach God like this. We cannot imagine what it is like to be God. We can try to meditate on aspects of God. Godliness, in the sense of our ever being God, will, quite simply, always elude us.

What we require is an approach. The one we shall use is to walk with these women. We are meeting God in Jesus through them because we acknowledge our distance in time and space from the events of his last hours. We cannot meet him there face to face. But Jesus did come into contact with these women. These encounters are captured in Scripture, myth or in pious tradition.

Whatever their source, they can be of use to us in prayer and meditation. We can use them to deepen our understanding of the gifts of God, which flow from the suffering of his son, Jesus Christ. By looking at these contacts with women, by hearing the words he said, by imagining their reactions, their feelings, we can come closer to Jesus. In that way we are more closely connected to the passion. We have a bridge to it. We can become one of the women. We can share their insight, their distress, their pain, their sympathy, their strength, their resolution.

These incidents also give us the opportunity to think about the nature of Jesus. We will see his love. We can receive his forgiveness. We can feel acceptance, as women did in his company. We can put ourselves in the place of women to receive his healing. We will be challenged and confronted by Jesus.

These women on the way of the cross, the Via Dolorosa, encountered Jesus at a specific time. They met him just as we encounter Jesus in our lives specifically. We do not have a general wishy-washy saviour who, as the young American tourist might say, 'kind of, like, sort of, you know' encounters us. Nothing could be further from the truth. Each and every one of us has had, has, will continue to have, a specific contact with Jesus.

Women on the way of the cross can draw us deeper into our own contact with Jesus because these women did – do – have contacts of a close, specific, sometimes an almost intimate nature. That is why we will look at the passion through them. And by looking through their eyes, thinking on their contacts and through what is said to them, we can come into closer contact with Jesus. We can move into the action as Jesus proceeds on the way towards the saving actions of his death.

Yet it would be wrong to claim this as private property. By concentrating on specific women, we are commencing a corporate activity. Each person reading this book is doing so for themselves. But the words on the page are there for all to see. We may be engaged in a personal activity that also has a communal dimension. This is important. Our reactions, unique as they are, gain force when they are combined with others'. A solitary event has a wider impact.

Our meditations on women on the way realize this. We have acknowledged that the encounters between women and Jesus on the Via Dolorosa connect them to other events in the life, death and resurrection of Jesus. To that end, we will be always on the move. We will move forward to and back from the passion. One event may well take us far beyond itself. We will look to other incidents in the manifold ministry of Jesus. We will see him accept people. We will see him challenge others. We will see him make whole those in need of healing.

In doing so we associate ourselves with those who encountered Jesus. We are not remote from the gospel people. We are if we walk a solitary path. Unique experience is real. But the Christian experience is to seek to join others. It does not seek to cement a personal experience. It wants to stretch it. It has to be shared. We do that because we have the temerity to recognize that the Christ's revelation is beyond individual appropriation. Other people matter.

Jesus worked socially. That he did so should not surprise us. We are social beings. We are not alone. Our walk with women on the way of the cross can unite us with them. Through them we can move closer to Jesus. And, like those women, we can let others know how exciting such proximity can be. We do that in the belief that we are not remote from the passion.

The life, death and resurrection of Jesus was at a certain time and place. But faith is the element that allows us to transcend these restrictions. God is beyond time and space. If God was made manifest in Jesus at a specific place and time, it is the Church's duty to show how this manifestation has an impact beyond the historical period. We do that because we do not believe we have arrived. Or that we know the specific location of our own destination. We aspire to Godliness. We hope to live in God's presence. To do more would be arrogant. To claim success would be obscene. We try, not always successfully, to do it with humility. We do it acknowledging a simple hope. We too are on the way.

1

The woman with the alabaster jar

The first contact between a woman and Jesus to be mentioned in a passion narrative is something of a pointer. In many ways it is an incident that alerts us to much of what is to befall Jesus. It is also instructive because it involves a number of things that tell us about the sort of person Jesus was. Further, it tells us something about the social mores of those among whom he lived.

While this encounter gives us clues to aspects of the character of Jesus, it is also a foretaste of the misunderstandings, deceptions and agony involved in his death. This, just as all reading of Scripture and meditation upon it, has reverberations far and beyond the time of the recorded events. Likewise those misunderstandings and deceptions contained in the exchange can act as a trigger for us to think of those things that were – are – to befall those who profess faith in Jesus as the Christ.

Followers of Jesus, in trying to make the stories understandable, have sometimes confused events. At times they have put together either elements or complete stories that were, and should remain, separate. This amalgamation can sometimes combine themes and personalities that do

11

not fit. Some of this occurs with the woman with the alabaster jar.

If we are to proclaim faith in Jesus as the Christ, says the Church, we should try to become more like him. If this is to be within our grasp then this first incident involving a woman in the passion has ramifications for us now. It points to the need for us to look at how we relate to people. We will see how accepting Jesus was. We, in our imitation of Jesus, aspire to acceptance and tolerance. This acceptance does not rely on personal introductions. We do not need to know individuals' names to make them welcome. We can accept them as they are.

Jesus gives us a lead in this. He accepts those who are named as well as those whose names have been lost to time. He likewise accepts those who are known to be ill and those whose state of health is not given to us by the writers of the gospels.

The unknown woman

One powerful aspect of this first episode with a woman in the passion resides in her anonymity. It involves a woman whose name is not known. However, we do know the name of a man associated with her. The incident takes place in his home. The event occurs at Bethany in the house of Simon. Indeed, in the versions we read in the Gospels of Matthew and Mark we learn a little more than Simon's name. We are told he is a leper.

For people living in the West up until recently, leprosy brought with it many negative connotations. The segregation of lepers from those not affected by the disease was commonplace. This occurred in reality and in popular imagination. Missions to lepers, island colonies, personal isolation – these are aspects associated with leprosy. In recent years things have changed. It is hoped popular perception will fall into line with medical trends. In biblical times, however, those with the disease are mentioned as living within the community. Yet it still holds that, in many ways, lepers were outcasts. The fact that Jesus is in the house of a leper tells us that he is prepared to befriend those people who may have been rejected by his own society. Noting the illness of Simon also informs us that other pieces of reject humanity may be there. There is a more subversive element to all this. To associate with a leper can imply a rejection of the fitter and more conservative elements in the village. The evangelists do not mention the names of those present in the house apart from the host, Simon. The most startling member of the anonymous company was a woman.

It is worth pausing to look at how often Jesus deals with unnamed people in the course of his ministry. It is both a comfort and surprise to us to learn that Jesus accepted such folk and, in doing so, enraged and seemed to reject others who wanted to learn more about him and from him. This extends to those who receive the gift of healing from him. People could benefit from Jesus. They need not be in his immediate presence. Benefits could be gained even at a physical remove from him. One example capturing many of these elements is the story of the centurion's servant.

A centurion there had a slave whom he valued highly, and who was ill and close to death. When he heard about Jesus, he sent some Jewish elders to him, asking him to come and heal his slave. (Luke 7.2–3)

We do not learn the names of the people who appeal to Jesus on behalf of the likewise anonymous soldier, let alone that of the slave. Names can be helpful in giving authenticity to accounts. Often when people are telling stories about what they consider to be an extraordinary event they are challenged by others. A stock response, as telling of human nature as it is of the quest for veracity, is to ask them to give the name of a witness. Better still, ask them the names of the protagonists. That a named person was there lends credence to the account. The much vaunted urban myth stems from the perennially unnamed 'friend of a friend'. Investigation and challenge tend to come up with similar results. The person at the centre of the story is not known to the one relating the tale. Therefore, the so-called amazing incident probably did not occur.

In the story of the centurion and the slave, it is the response of Jesus to the message that is intriguing. The centurion has sent people who he thinks may be more acceptable to Jesus. But Jesus is told through them and others that the soldier does not have ideas above his station.

> And Jesus went with them, but when he was not far from the house, the centurion sent friends to say to him, 'Lord, do not trouble yourself, for I am not worthy to have you come under my roof; therefore I did not presume to come to you. But only speak the word, and let my servant be healed.' (Luke 7.6–7)

Rewards for faith

This faith is rewarded. The slave is restored to health. This centurion has been well remembered since the writing of the gospels despite the lack of a name. His words, or a variation upon them, are often used in response to the invitation to receive communion during the celebration of the eucharist. Such is our regard for the healing power of the Christ. Likewise is our realization that we can neither demand nor deserve such healing. Yet it is freely given.

So it is with the woman with the alabaster jar. Anonymity and reward for faith are two features in the story of what occurs in the house of Simon the leper. The accounts in Matthew and Mark are similar in many ways. A woman carrying an alabaster jar comes to Jesus in Simon's house. It is worth taking note of what she carries. This alabaster jar was to become Mary Magdalene's in the cult that was built up around the saint. It is a symbol you can use to recognize Mary Magdalene in paintings and stained glass windows. It is, however, the rightful property of another woman.

> While he was at Bethany in the house of Simon the leper, as he sat at the table, a woman came with an alabaster jar of very costly ointment of nard, and she broke open the jar and poured the ointment on his head. (Mark 14.3)

Some translations of the Bible inform us that the ointment was pure nard. Nard is an aromatic balsam. It is curious that the author of Mark's Gospel thought it was important to let us know what was in the jar but not the name of the person carrying it. Ointment is something applied to the skin, although we tend to think of it having a medicinal use. The modern reader can impute some attempt at healing to the woman's action. We are told that the ointment, having a medical use or not, is costly. And much is made of the cost.

But some were there who said to one another in anger, 'Why was the ointment wasted in this way? For this ointment might have been sold for more than three hundred denarii, and the money given to the poor.' (Mark 14.4)

If we accept scholars' calculations that a denarius was the equivalent of a labourer's wage for one day, the ointment is precious indeed. In John's Gospel the figure of three hundred denarii comes from the mouth of Judas Iscariot. That this is so is no accident. John goes some way to emphasize that the motives of Judas are far from honourable.

(He said this not because he cared for the poor, but because he was a thief; he kept the common purse and used to steal what was put into it.) (John 12.5–6)

In Mark's and Matthew's accounts, the woman pours the flask of oil over the head of Jesus. We have noted that there are objections. This ointment is worth money. It could be sold. The money could be given to the poor. Jesus replies with an uncomfortable truth. The poor, the very people his Jewish tradition has said must be cared for and protected, are a constant feature of existence. This does not mean that we are freed from the responsibility we have to the poor. It is about opportunities.

'For you will always have the poor with you, and you can show kindness to them whenever you wish; but you will not always have me.' (Mark 14.7)

Having dealt with the critics, Jesus declares the woman's action of anointing him beautiful. He says she has acted to the utmost of her capability. It was not an action done for the poor. It was for him alone.

'She has done what she could; she has anointed my body beforehand for its burial.' (Mark 14.8)

Anointing for burial is an ancient custom. Various cultures have prepared the dead for journeys from this world to the next, however the peoples might have understood that. But anointing in anticipation of a burial, more especially when the living recipient acknowledges what is going on, is startling. Not surprisingly, the people in the company of Jesus are shocked. He is seen to be predicting his death, almost glorying in it, and accepting this gesture that alerts us that what is to follow will be bleak, painful and grim.

This anointing in advance of death is enshrined in the Church's practice of anointing the sick. In parts of the Church such a practice is defined sacramentally. Nowadays there is widespread acceptance of the practice of anointing. It could be argued that this has gone too far, reducing a potent Christian symbol to little more than a pleasurable and possibly meaningless tactile experience. Oil is or can be used in key Christian ceremonies – baptism, confirmation, ordination or anointing of the sick. This latter use can be used to great effect in the ministry of healing. People seeking wholeness of body or spirit may be anointed during a service designated for healing, or during or after special prayers. It is only relatively recently that anointing has reverted to such broader uses than that captured in the old title of Extreme Unction. The anointing of the seriously ill – and such anointing was reserved for people in grave danger – was considered a rite of passage for those near death. Anointing has a solid scriptural basis.

Are any among you suffering? They should pray. Are any cheerful? They should sing songs of praise. Are any among you sick? They should call for the elders of the church and have them pray over them, anointing them with oil in the name of the Lord. The prayer of faith will save the sick, and the Lord will raise them up; and anyone who has committed sins will be forgiven. (James 5.13–15)

However solid a basis it has, this practice can have unfortunate, rather than the hoped for miraculous, results. A priest in north London tells the story of how the family of a man requested the vicar to call by. The purpose of the visit was made clear. The priest was to pray over and anoint the man whom the family believed to be near death. The priest says he called at the house, was ushered into the room where the man was sitting up in bed reading a newspaper. The man looked up and exclaimed, 'God! I must be *really* ill if they've called you!'

There is a much more serious intent to the words of Jesus in response to those gathered in Simon's house. He is predicting events that those around him will witness but do not realize are soon to be set in train. This mixed company does not or cannot grasp the implication of his comments. But Jesus accepts a gift from a woman that is a token of his own future pain. He allows her to make an offering. Jesus is loving and accepting. We know this from other incidents recorded in the gospels. His dealings with the poor and outcast, the sick, with sinners, all tell us of his acceptance of people in, despite and because of their shortcomings.

A new order

The encounters of Jesus with women and children likewise

18

tell us of his acceptance of people despite their status in the social order. Despite the independence some women may have enjoyed in the broader community and especially in the company of Jesus, they are often relegated to the sidelines. They feature as almost an afterthought in the reported count of those miraculously fed by Jesus. Children are further relegated to the fringe. They could be viewed as dangerous. They were to be kept at bay. Or so the disciples thought. Their actions were to receive a firm rebuke from Jesus.

> People were bringing even infants to him that he might touch them; and when the disciples saw it, they sternly ordered them not to do it. But Jesus called for them and said, 'Let the little children come to me, and do not stop them; for it is to such as these that the kingdom of God belongs.' (Luke 18.15–17)

There is a yet deeper aspect to the acceptance of Jesus. It resides in forgiveness. The anointing of Jesus by the woman is met with his startling declaration of the forgiveness of sins. In his epistle James espouses emulation of this after having advocated prayer and anointing.

> Therefore confess your sins to one another, and pray for one another, so that you may be healed. The prayer of the righteous is powerful and effective. (James 5.16)

The healing action of the Church, which attempts to mirror the healing ministry of Jesus, is both an individual and a corporate one. The healing of one person is for the benefit not only of the individual concerned but also of the broader community. There can be an unhelpful concentration on individual cures to the exclusion of their social context. It echoes the dangers of personal religion

19

at the expense of the corporate church experience. The forgiveness of sins of one person within the Church is to the betterment of the health of the entire Church. This is the overriding social importance of the ministry of reconciliation and healing. To fence it off for individual and personal benefit is to divorce it from the common life of the Church. Saint Paul warned of the dangers of such thinking. His coining of the image of the body tells us that the health or malady of one member cannot but affect the whole. This is by virtue of being part of a whole.

> Indeed, the body does not consist of one member but of many. If the foot would say, 'Because I am not a hand, I do not belong to the body,' that would not make it any less a part of the body. And if the ear would say, 'Because I am not an eye, I do not belong to the body,' that would not make it any less a part of the body. If the whole body were an eye, where would the hearing be? If the whole body were hearing, where would the sense of smell be? But as it is, God arranged the members in the body, each one of them, as he chose. If all were a single member, where would the body be? As it is, there are many members, yet one body. (1 Corinthians 12.14–20)

The background or social status of someone in the Church should not matter. It is not without interest that the parallel of the incident concerning the woman with the alabaster jar in Luke's Gospel does not happen in the home of a leper. It occurs in the house of someone with a more exalted place in society. Yet the name Simon is constant.

One of the Pharisees asked Jesus to eat with him, and he

went into the Pharisee's house and took his place at the table. And a woman in the city, who was a sinner, having learned that he was eating in the Pharisee's house, brought an alabaster jar of ointment. (Luke 7.36–7)

What follows is an extraordinary outpouring of grief and emotion. The woman does what can be interpreted as a tactile form of confession. Instead of saying what she has done to rupture her relationship with God, she physically displays her contrition.

She stood behind him at his feet, weeping, and began to bathe his feet with her tears and to dry them with her hair. Then she continued kissing his feet and anointing them with the ointment. (Luke 7.38)

This gives rise to a curious exchange. Simon the Pharisee wonders how Jesus can be a prophet and not know the character of the woman touching him. She is well known to be a sinner. There is an intriguing question that does not appear in the text, one of those puzzles we encounter from time to time when we read the Bible. It is all well and good for the Pharisee to wonder at Jesus's lack of prophetic credentials. But if Simon objects so much to the presence of such a woman near his table, what is she doing in his house in the first place? The question is not asked and so is never addressed. Jesus is more concerned with the individual ministering to him than with such quibbles. He accepts her offering and reciprocates with a huge gift. He forgives her sins. To explain this Jesus tells a story of debt. The difference between fifty and five hundred denarii is crucial – the bigger the debt the creditor writes off the greater the thanks in the heart of the debtor. Simon himself acknowledges this and Jesus commends him for his insight. But having first commended him, Jesus proceeds to rebuke him. In a beautiful series of contrasts, he places the welcome of Simon the Pharisee against that of the unnamed woman. It is the woman who is indirectly praised for her various actions to Jesus. They all involve his feet. She bathes them with tears. She kisses them and anoints them with oil. Simon, on the other hand, did nothing to approach this. Jesus moves on from this analysis of his reception to something greater.

> 'Therefore, I tell you, her sins, which were many, have been forgiven; hence she has shown great love. But the one to whom little is forgiven, loves little.' Then he said to her, 'Your sins are forgiven.' (Luke 7.47–8)

Think of what the woman must have felt. Recognized, even vilified, as a sinner by people gathered in the house, she is congratulated by Jesus for her actions. She has the privilege of touching the Christ. Her hands rub her own tears into his feet. She hears forgiveness pronounced. She may even feel the proverbial weight of her past lifted from her shoulders. Tears of relief replace tears of contrition. The coda to this incident is one often repeated by Jesus.

> And he said to the woman, 'Your faith has saved you; go in peace.' (Luke 7.50)

If the woman is so great a sinner, as we are told, she is both accepted and forgiven. She is accepted into the presence of the Christ. He graciously receives her ministrations and points to their inner meaning. He then gives freedom from her past. He sees her in a positive light. It is one of love.

This outpouring of forgiveness and love is likewise

22

extended to us. We can mirror her actions by taking our sins to the Christ and being prepared for the revolutionary acceptance he extends. We can take our faults and failures to him and be forgiven. We can and should do this as a group. Every service of holy communion involves the confession and absolution of sins. We can highlight this within a special service of reconciliation. Or we may choose to avail ourselves of sacramental confession and absolution on a one-to-one basis with a priest. The effect is the same. We are able to take the risk of allowing our faith to be rewarded. We too can be made whole. We too can go in peace.

A woman named

There remains one other account in the gospels that should not be avoided. It also occurs in Bethany. It is just before Jesus makes his triumphal entry into Jerusalem. But unlike what we have seen in Matthew, Mark and Luke, the participants of this episode in the Gospel of John are named. It is the name of this woman that has been used by some to suggest that the woman with the alabaster jar is Mary Magdalene. Again, the only explanation for this is a misdirected effort to combine the gospel accounts.

The author of John's Gospel gives the name Mary to a woman who washes the feet of Jesus. It is not just any woman called Mary. The author goes some way to identify her in detail. She is the sister of Lazarus and Martha. It is the same Mary who ran to Jesus on the way to the tomb of Lazarus, declaring that her brother would not have died if the Lord had come earlier. The incident is contained in the chapter following the bringing of Lazarus back to life.

Six days before the Passover Jesus came to Bethany, the home of Lazarus, whom he had raised from the dead. There they gave a dinner for him. Martha served, and Lazarus was one of those at the table with him. Mary took a pound of costly perfume made of pure nard, anointed Jesus' feet, and wiped them with her hair. The house was filled with the fragrance of the perfume. (John 12.1–3)

Here are ingredients for confusion: the name of Mary, the ointment of nard, the feet of Jesus and the woman's wiping of them with her hair. Yet this is a named woman who is clearly not Mary Magdalene. In the house of Mary, sister of Lazarus and Martha, Jesus again accepts a gift. We have seen in the other stories that Jesus forgives. There is a similarity to be drawn from the three stories. Jesus accepts people as they are and then he extends to them his power to change their lives. Forgiveness is the radical tool of change. It is an extraordinary method of acceptance. It is a way of our becoming more like the Christ.

Compare this with Jesus's dealings with the high and mighty. Often those in authority are challenged by Jesus. Likewise, the rich are asked to look to the responsibilities their wealth carries with it. Forgiveness is not withheld from such people, but he makes them realize they are not immune from his call to examine their personal and public personae. He discomforts them. He challenges them. He rebukes them. But he does not do so out of spite, nor is his impetus petty jealousy. He does so to remind those who may see themselves as superior to others that real power is in God.

When Jesus is with the wealthy he reminds them of what the Jewish law requires in the arena of social affairs:

that those who find themselves in the positions they do should be careful of the sick, the poor, the needy and the outcast. The scriptures are packed with reminders to those who have to ensure that they care for those who have not. A quick glance at a biblical concordance will also show that Jesus too spoke of the responsibilities of wealth.

If we change Simon from the Pharisee back into the leper, we still learn from the example of Jesus. In the house of a leper we see Jesus doing just what he tells others to do. He is accepting the outcast sinner in the same way he accepts the hospitality of his diseased host. They are equal. He responds to each in a complete way. He accepts with wholeness.

We are not immune from the implications of this story. For a Christian there is a compelling reason to look at these incidents. We too need to look at how we respond to other people. We must continually assess our reaction to other people. We must pause and see how we react to other sinners. If we are to emulate Jesus – and this is a constant theme in the preaching of the faith of Christianity – we cannot afford to condemn those who do not live up to our ideals. More importantly, we should be looking to ourselves to see whether *we* live up to them. It is too easy for a Christian to denounce the behaviour of another person. What code do we use if we do this? Have we become the petty legalists that Jesus himself was so keen to confront? Better for us to look at the really difficult behaviour – our own. Such action brings us face to face with the oft cast-off realization that a Christian must acknowledge. That is that we, too, are sinners.

'Do not judge, so that you may not be judged. For with the judgment you make you will be judged, and the

measure you give will be the measure you get.'
(Matthew 7.1–2)

This is a warning of discomfiting equality. Jesus is
pointing to a reciprocity of action and reward. It is not in
the assessing of how other people fare that his followers
will be rewarded. Rather, it is how they act. The commonplace that action speaks louder than words was never more
compelling.

'Why do you see the speck in your neighbour's eye, but
do not notice the log in your own eye? Or how can you
say to your neighbour, "Let me take the speck out of
your eye," while the log remains in your own eye? You
hypocrite, first take the log out of your own eye, and
then you will see clearly to take the speck out of your
neighbour's eye.' (Matthew 7.3–5)

This is practical advice. Jesus is cautioning us to look to
ourselves. By realistically looking to our faults, we can be
freed to be of service to others. By accepting that we are
not perfect, we can proceed in service with a measure of
humility. We are freed to do what we can, not what we
think we would like to do. This constant acceptance shown
by Jesus is as disturbing to us as it was to those who heard
him speak.

Gifts and responsibilities

The challenge of Jesus was not only for those who did not
consider themselves upright. It also extended to those who
had received the good things of life. The Jewish tradition
stresses that such gifts do not come without responsibilities.
We cannot distance ourselves from these challenges and

responsibilities by an appeal to the passage of time. If we have a lion's share of the good things of this world, we need to ask ourselves some questions. Are we generous with what we have? Do we use our wealth for the benefit of others?

Such questions are bracing. They are as pertinent as those we asked ourselves of our own behaviour. Indeed, what we do with our riches is very much a question of how we behave. What do we do with our money is as necessary a question as how do we accept the outcast. Do we look after the poor and needy? The answers to these questions can be uncomfortable no matter what the passage of time. They are as challenging today as they were then.

All these issues are rightly raised by the reaction of Jesus to an anonymous woman in the house of a man named Simon in the village of Bethany. Yet there still remains a twist in the tale. You will recall that it is Judas who reminds us of the poor. But Jesus accepts this rich gift, almost sidelining the poor when Judas speaks. A beautiful thing, in which the woman, Jesus says, is doing all she can. He accepts the gift with love. And he tells everyone he is going to die.

> 'She has done what she could; she has anointed my body beforehand for its burial. Truly I tell you, wherever the good news is proclaimed in the whole world, what she has done will be told in remembrance of her.' (Mark 14.8–9)

In accepting the gift of anointing, Jesus accepts more than the gift. He accepts his fate. With this nameless woman he shares his pain, his anguish, his death. It is an act of acceptance of all of us. Jesus, in his passion, comes into the house of us when we are outcast. He is there to accept gifts, not for the sake of them, but he accepts them because in his death he will act for us.

Jesus accepts people as they are. He takes on board who we are with all our faults and he transcends them for us. By giving Jesus our faults, our failings, our sin, they can be changed. They can be forgiven. That is what the passion ultimately tells us. And in all these stories, divergent, conflicting as they may be, we are urged to do one thing: to enter into the place of that woman. For, like that woman, we can be accepted and can be forgiven. We are alerted to this in the pouring of oil by a nameless woman in a house at Bethany.

— 2 —

Veronica

The second woman to meet Jesus as he walks the way of
the cross is Veronica. This can be a very potent encounter.
Yet there may be reservations about this woman. The first
thing we have to recognize about her is a signal for much
of what is to follow. It is a simple admission: at no point
does the name Veronica appear in the gospel accounts of
the passion of Jesus. Indeed, the name does not appear in
the Bible at all.

For all this, Veronica is famous. She is more than
famous. Veronica is a saint. The Church is believed to have
bestowed sainthood upon her sometime before the tenth
century. The exact date is not known. She is commemo-
rated, or can be, on July 12 – a festival probably best
noted for its non-observance. She does not feature in
Anglican lectionaries. Veronica retains her sainthood
through the processes of the Roman Catholic Church
because of what the Holy See calls an Approved Cult. An
Approved Cult grows from a belief that veneration can, in
some cases, make up for the lack of evidence of a saint's
existence.

Perhaps this can be illustrated in Britain by the dedication of ancient churches. If you have travelled in the West Country of England or throughout Wales you can come across churches bearing the names of saints you may never have heard of. Your curiosity may well be stimulated. In some cases this might lead to research, which may lead in turn to frustration – you could well be disappointed if you were to consult a reference book of saints. That is simply because some of the saints are not listed in such books. Yet there remains a problem: there is still the church you have visited that is dedicated to someone bearing the honorific of 'Saint'.

Do you know anything about Saint Gastyn? He is even more mysterious than Veronica. Unlike her, Gastyn was never put through the process of being formally canonized. Despite this, Gastyn is still the patron saint of a church in a village in Powys, Llangasty-Talyllyn, that takes his name. There is an entertaining mind game here. Because the church bears his name, surely there was such a saint. How else did he come to be the patron of the church? It can be argued that there must have been such a saint. Otherwise to whom is the church dedicated? This argument can seem circular but it helps to protect a local tradition in the face of concerted, seemingly more rational, opposition. The Roman Catholic Church may point to what it deems a Popular Cult, a step short of an Approved Cult. It notes the veneration of a local worthy. It may even attempt to substitute the word 'blessed' for 'saint'. In the end, it acknowledges that many people will persist in using the arguably misgained title of Saint. This may be the case for Saint Gastyn.

Veronica, however, has something of a stronger case. She is classified as a saint because of an Approved Cult. An Approved Cult comes out in support of tradition and pious observation rather than relying on academic, some might say objective, analysis.

So Veronica is famous. She is famous for a contact with Jesus that is firmly enshrined in tradition. It is a contact portrayed in the stations of the cross. Like the dedication of churches to relatively obscure saints, from time to time people have criticized the observance of the stations of the cross. They object to this religious practice because of what they see as the lack of biblical evidence for some of it. These accusations have often cited Veronica. We cannot draw back from this. It is best encountered by a simple admission: Veronica is famous for something that may never have happened. If we wanted to push her case we could take a rather simplistic contrary view. Maybe it did happen. There is as much evidence to support this view as its opposite, so it could have happened. But then, as we have admitted, maybe it did not. Either way, it must be honestly conceded that there is little evidence to support either claim.

We can exhaust ourselves in efforts to try to prove or disprove some matters in religious tradition. In prayer and meditation it can sometimes be helpful to put to one side the factual. We free ourselves to see what tradition or imagination may be leading us to consider. This is the basis of much imaginative prayer. It allows us to use our creative gifts to deepen our understanding of events recorded in Scripture or apocryphal stories. For that reason alone Veronica can be fruitfully considered, because the vital part of the contact she is said to have had with Jesus does not reside in whether or not it actually occurred. What is important is what the incident expresses. Veronica is renowned as a saint for the action she is portrayed as carrying out. This is the basis of the sixth station of the cross. In this station Veronica meets Jesus on the road to his execution.

The trials begin

Up to the third station Jesus Christ is portrayed as a victim. Things are done against him and to him. The progression of the stations of the cross starts with Jesus being condemned to death by Pontius Pilate. This action does not come out of the blue. Pilate has attempted to stave off mob rule. He knows he is not equal to the task. Pilate says the man is innocent of the charges against him. He goes further than that. Pilate says he can find no crime against Jesus. This is in stark contrast to the view of the people who have accused him.

> Pilate, wanting to release Jesus, addressed them again; but they kept shouting 'Crucify, crucify him!' A third time he said to them, 'Why, what evil has he done? I found in him no ground for the sentence of death. I will therefore have him flogged and then release him.' (Luke 23.20–22)

The gospels do not agree on the precise sequence of events. Yet they do agree that Jesus is subjected to verbal and physical abuse. He is beaten by the soldiers. He is scourged. He is dressed in a 'king's' robe and taunted. A crown of thorns is placed on his head. He is pushed, shoved and struck. After suffering these indignities he is again brought before the crowd. Pilate is seeking to plant seeds of pity. He hopes they might see Jesus as he does. Perhaps he can elicit sympathy from the crowd. This feeling for a fellow being would not only move them, they would be shocked into realizing that Jesus had been wrongly accused. Pilate's efforts are wasted. The plan fails.

> But they kept urgently demanding with loud shouts that he should be crucified; and their voices prevailed. (Luke 23.23)

Frustrated justice becomes political expediency. To keep the peace, to allay his critics, for a range of considerations we can only guess at, Pontius Pilate allows Jesus to go to his death. Having been through this merry-go-round of 'justice', Jesus accepts his fate and takes up the cross. It is worth exercising a little caution here. There is a risk that this resignation can be overplayed. It can seem that Jesus, a man who has shown himself to be a challenging and confronting teacher, becomes a malleable tool in the drama. We must bear in mind his prayers in the garden of Gethsemane.

> 'My Father, if it is possible, let this cup pass from me; yet not what I want but what you want.' (Matthew 26.39)

This is not a facile acceptance of what was to happen but a bringing of his human will into line with Godly will. It is a making whole – man and God in the Christ – that sets these events in train.

The way of the cross

Now Jesus is to carry the instrument of his own torture and death. Artists often render this scene with Jesus displaying an attitude of resolution. He accepts his fate with determination. The Christ takes the weight of the tree upon which he will ultimately hang. For all this apparent stoic resignation, we must not construe this as acceptance of some easy task. It is one only achieved at great personal cost. Yet it does bring a universal pay-off. The Church celebrates the passion because it tells the story of God's perfect love through God's suffering for God's creation. These actions lead to liberation. But that is to jump ahead of ourselves somewhat. The stations of the cross dramatize this slow walk to our freedom, which underlines the suffering through which that freedom is achieved. That is their attraction. They give a focus to meditation. They are a step-by-step mental re-enactment that reminds us that our freedom was not without price.

Having accepted the cross, Jesus suffers the first of three falls on the way to Golgotha. He meets his mother. This is a turning point in the chain of events. The victim, the suffering Jesus, now encounters the woman who bore him. It is an encounter redolent with poignancy and pain. It can and should be a touchstone for profound prayer and meditation. We will consider that meeting, along with other contacts between the mother and her son, in another chapter. Suffice it to say at this point that the victim is seen through different eyes.

It is at this juncture that the course of events changes. Something is being done for the Christ. His load is temporarily eased. It is taken by Simon of Cyrene. This is not a moment of heroic championing of the underdog by an individual. It is not the triumph many of us would like it to be. Simon would probably have preferred to remain what he was up to that point, an anonymous spectator. Pulled from the crowd, he is forced to carry the Christ's cross. Because of this participation, he becomes a named party. This man from foreign parts is clearly identified.

They compelled a passer-by, who was coming in from the country, to carry his cross; it was Simon of Cyrene, the father of Alexander and Rufus. (Mark 15.21)

Simon is reluctant to set to his task. He does so because he is made to. Jesus walks behind him. There seems little chance of conversation. The condemned man looks at the cross as it goes before him. He does so knowing that he will die upon it. He is also aware that he must soon take up its weight again. Simon of Cyrene has completed his cameo appearance in the drama. Jesus embraces the cross again.

Then comes another encounter. It is a meeting of sufferer and spectator. Yet this spectator is different. She gets involved in a different way. Veronica turns the tide of events. Unlike Simon of Cyrene's, Veronica's is a contact of touch and of free will. It is something that speaks without words. A man weighed down by torture and abuse is staggering along. His face is covered in sweat, dirt and blood. He is in pain. And from the crowd steps a woman who puts a cloth to his face and wipes it clean.

There are a number of possible interpretations to be put on this action. Let us think of just two. The first is that Veronica has carried out an action that has the support of others. Her compassion is shared by all those around her. The woman steps out from the crowd. The people about her, the soldiers in charge, even Jesus himself, allow her to do so. She steps forward and wipes clean Jesus's face. Again they all allow it to happen. It is a singular activity that has corporate support. It is something that allows the pain, anguish and despair Jesus is suffering to be alleviated. He does not face his fate alone. His situation is shared, albeit for the slightest of moments.

What's in a name?

What do we know of the name given to this woman? Veronica is the name of a herb. The common name for this herb is speedwell. Its Latin name, the international botanical name, is *Veronica officinalis*. It is described by one herbalist, Juliette de Baïracli Levy in *The Illustrated Herbal Handbook* (Faber & Faber, London, 1982), as being found in pastures and copses. Pastures are places of grazing. We still tend to think, despite the more sinister aspects of intensive farming today, of relaxed, contented animals grazing. There is the now commonplace expression 'sheep may safely graze'. The line comes in the English translation of Pales's aria from Johann Sebastian Bach's Secular Cantata Number 8. It is a snippet that becomes the title of the aria. So we can think of the herb growing in a place of openness and contentment. But the herbalist tells us it can be more intimate than that. A copse can be a little place of refuge. Shielded from the busy paths and byways, there is a suggestion of privacy. It is a place apart. Or a copse can be an undergrowth. Whatever the setting, this herb is grown in a safe place.

This combination of calm, safety and healing suggested by the name of a herb is embodied in Veronica's action. It is caught in the extension of an arm holding a cloth as it goes towards the face of Jesus. The suffering of Jesus is transcended within a second. The pain is transformed into an intimate moment of caring. A gesture of kindness is extended to a fellow human being in pain.

Levy also tells us that the flower of the herb speedwell is small and delicate. The plant is hardy but its flower is fragile. This contrast can apply to Veronica. There is a discrepancy between the gesture of reaching out to the suffering Jesus and what it may signify. This is the second interpretation of what Veronica does. It is the opposite of the joint compassion illustrated above. Instead of an action that has the agreement and support of others in the crowd and those taking part in the executionary procession, Veronica acts alone. Her reaching out becomes a brave, almost brazen, action. Drawing on her reserves of courage, she overcomes her fears and steps out in defiance of the troops. They turn to stop her. People in the crowd attempt to restrain her. By her persistence, she confronts and gently overpowers them. Why does she do this? It is still a generous gesture. By taking on the power of the guards and by defying the mob's acquiescence to what the procession is leading to, Veronica allows her singular compassion to be the victor. Having stepped out of line, she can now give solace, comfort and relief to the suffering Christ. The fruit of her action is almost the antithesis of it – through the strong action comes gentleness.

Speedwell, the herbalist tells us, is a minute herb with remarkable medicinal powers that seem far out of proportion to its size. Likewise, this action of Veronica's can be seen as a tiny effort that has a momentous effect. Her defiance is an attempt at healing. It is, however, a healing that cannot be effective. It cannot be because, despite the efforts of those who sympathize with Jesus in his plight, his course is unalterable. His fate is irreversible. We have seen that in the resolution expressed in his prayers in the garden of Gethsemane. This is his inner resolve. But there are external factors that also contribute to the impotence of Veronica's action. Jesus has suffered too much already to be able to take advantage of her healing efforts. They cannot undo the damage already done. He is nearly worn out by what he has already suffered. And there is yet more to come. For all this, we should not discard Veronica's motive even if we do consider her actions doomed to failure.

In the action of wiping his face, Veronica extends something valuable to Jesus. It is a compound of love, care and concern. It combines these elements in an affinity for the suffering victim. And by doing so it defies everything else going on around them.

De Baïracli Levy tells us the herb is noted for its power to remove mucus from the body. It is reputed to be efficacious in soothing internal tissues. Using what we are told about the herb, we can impute a physical and spiritual aspect to the name of this woman, Veronica. Her action is one of attempted healing. Healing is more than applying a remedy to a hurt or disease. There is a larger aspect to it. Healing is the making whole of a person. It brings people to completeness. It fills the void of those who are lacking in body or spirit. By doing so, it brings these elements that are sometimes thought of as diverse into unity and harmony. Healing, wholeness, goes against the traditional false divide of body and spirit. Healing leads us to consider them as unified. Healing brings body and spirit together.

Yet the real triumph in the tragedy of the passion of the Christ is not in what is done for him. Neither is the victory in what is done to him. The ultimate triumph and victory for Christians is what is done by him. That is because Jesus Christ is the ultimate whole being. Jesus is not only human, he is God – the man accepting this gesture of kindness from Veronica is God. Jesus leads us to himself. The passion and death of Jesus lead us to God. The Christ's suffering leads to a wholeness extended to all humanity. That is why we treasure Jesus and the passion. It is a healing action for all people in all places for all time.

Let us turn Veronica's gesture back in on itself. The immobilized recipient of her care is the same man who was once active in the healing of so many others. He was more than active in these cures, he was vital to them. Consider for a moment some of the miraculous cures Jesus brought about. He healed the lame so that they could walk again. He restored sight to the blind. He restored to people faculties they had lost through illness, disease and accident. And he did even more than that – he gave people abilities they had never had.

The blind see

This is best expressed in the extended passage in John's Gospel in which Jesus gave sight to a man who had never had it. This miracle was so amazing that the evangelist gives over almost an entire chapter to it. In chapter nine, the writer of John reports in some detail what transpired. It is given a literary foretaste in chapter eight when Jesus makes one of his seven poetic declarations in the Gospel of John. These are known as the 'I am sayings'.

Again Jesus spoke to them saying, 'I am the light of the world. Whoever follows me will never walk in darkness but will have the light of life.' (John 8.12)

This saying leads to an argument with and among the Pharisees. In that argument Jesus is unable to satisfy his opponents, who want to differentiate between God and the man Jesus. Jesus is telling them that no differentiation is necessary. He tells them what the Christian faith declares: that he and the Father are one.

So Jesus said, 'When you have lifted up the Son of Man,

then you will realise that I am he, and that I do nothing on my own, but I speak these things as the Father has instructed me.' (John 8.28)

After escaping the wrath of the Pharisees, who want to stone him, Jesus passes a man who has never seen. There is a discussion as to the cause of the blindness. The problem is stated and is followed by a direct question. Someone's sin has led to this. Was it the sin of the parents or of the man himself? Jesus dismisses this suggestion. Neither the man nor his parents sinned. Jesus mixes a salve from dirt and his spit, and puts the paste on the eyes of the blind man. Sending the man to wash in a pool, Jesus awaits his return. The man does as he has been bade and returns. Now he can see.

The healing causes a furore. Neighbours are astounded at the change in the man. But there is more to it than that. Jesus's healing actions occurred on the sabbath. He has breached the fourth commandment.

Controversy engulfs the now sighted man and his parents. All three are brought before the Pharisees to answer questions. The man's mother is put to the test. The man claiming the cure cannot be the child she bore. Such a claim is rejected. The parents confirm that he is their son. They state that he was blind from birth. In an attempt to keep sin as a factor, the Pharisees move the blame from the blind man or his parents to an outsider. They attempt to shift the blame onto Jesus. Jesus had denied that anyone had sinned. So it must be Jesus who is the sinner. When asked by the Pharisees if he knows that Jesus is a sinner, the once blind man says

'I do not know whether he is a sinner. One thing I do know, that though I was blind, now I see.' (John 9.25)

This healing of the man born blind was one of many different cures. Jesus cured lepers. He drove out demons. The insane were restored to their right mind. The unwell became whole. Lost faculties were returned. Handicaps were overcome. These are extraordinary stories. They are complete cures.

Who was Veronica?

Some versions of the myths surrounding Veronica attempt to give her a scriptural basis. This is a dubious exercise. It fails because it attempts to turn a woman mentioned in Scripture into another enshrined in pious tradition. Yet in our imaginative meditation, we see Veronica become someone who is trying to return to the Christ what she herself has gained. That version suggests that Veronica is the woman who had been cured of the issue of blood. Having been made whole, she is seeking to reflect the love Jesus had displayed to her.

> Now there was a woman who had been suffering from haemorrhages for twelve years. She had endured much under many physicians, and she had spent all that she had; and she was no better, but rather grew worse. (Mark 5.26)

In that verse of Scripture we are given the picture of one who has little to lose. Her long pitched battle with illness continues, and she could be forgiven for losing hope. But the news of the miracle worker has filled her with hope. This is faith.

She had heard about Jesus, and came up behind him in

41

the crowd and touched his cloak, for she said, 'If I but touch his clothes I will be made well.' (Mark 5.27–8)

It is this combination of faith and fabric that is used to turn this woman into Veronica. These are mere externals. There is an imagined depth beyond the exterior signs. The woman had faith that was rewarded. It was rewarded in an amazing, almost frightening manner.

Immediately her haemorrhage stopped; and she felt in her body that she was healed of her disease. (Mark 5.29)

This is health. This is wholeness. The woman's faith has given her spiritual health. Expressing her faith by reaching out to touch the cloak of Jesus restored her to physical health. It is this balance of spirit and body that is essential to the healing power of Jesus. Jesus is aware that she has been made whole. He has felt the power leave him. He wants to know who touched him. The woman is initially too scared to come forward but eventually does so. Having been rewarded with a physical cure, Jesus now rewards her trust.

But the woman, knowing what had happened to her, came in fear and trembling, fell down before him, and told him the whole truth. He said to her, 'Daughter, your faith has made you well; go in peace, and be healed of your disease.' (Mark 5.33–4)

The reward for faith can make us think of the other kinds of healing. These are signified by words so often used by Jesus to make it clear that his power is even greater than the mere physical, astounding as that is in itself. Jesus also made people whole through the forgiveness of their sins.

42

Let us look at one example, the healing of the paralytic in the ninth chapter of Matthew's Gospel. Jesus notices something more profound than one person's malady. That is why he hesitates before giving the physical cure.

When Jesus saw their faith, he said to the paralytic, 'Take heart, son; your sins are forgiven.' (Matthew 9.2)

A great dispute arises. The scribes think Jesus is blaspheming.

But Jesus, perceiving their thoughts, said, 'Why do you think evil in your hearts? For which is easier to say, "Your sins are forgiven", or to say "Stand up and walk"?' (Matthew 9.5)

It is only then that Jesus gives a physical cure to the paralysed man. He says he is doing so to give the doubters faith. Initially Jesus looked to the spiritual well-being of the man. It is only after he has addressed that that he gives him the capacity to walk. Jesus sees what is required in a person and gives it to them. That is the key to being healed. The healings of Jesus are about making people whole. They are more – much, much more – than physical cures.

Completeness was also extended to the woman who washed his feet. It comes in the form of absolution.

'Therefore, I tell you, her sins, which were many, have been forgiven; hence she has shown great love. But the one to whom little is forgiven, loves little.' Then he said, 'Your sins are forgiven.' (Luke 7.47–8)

Those around Jesus begin to question each other.

But those who were at the table with him began to say among themselves, 'Who is this, who even forgives sins?' (Luke 7.49)

Jesus does not respond to the questions of those around him but chooses instead to speak again to the woman. He speaks to the now healed. The message is the same as it was to the woman who had had the issue of blood.

And he said to the woman, 'Your faith has saved you. Go in peace.' (Luke 7.50)

This forgiveness is clearly paralleled in the story of the woman taken in adultery, found at the beginning of the eighth chapter of the Gospel of John. Having challenged the woman's accusers, Jesus is left alone with her. No stone has been thrown. No one is without sin.

Jesus straightened up and said to her, 'Woman, where are they? Has no one condemned you?' She said, 'No one, sir'. And Jesus said, 'Neither do I condemn you. Go on your way and from now on, do not sin again.' (John 8.10–11)

All these incidents speak of the healing strength of Jesus. When we consider his active ministry we see Jesus doing these things, bringing people to wholeness, physically and spiritually, in the face of opposition and much to the alarm of those around him.

Yet here, as we pause with Veronica as she steps forward with her cloth on the road to Golgotha, Jesus seems pitiable and weak, bereft of the power that made people well, whole and forgiven. But, if we really thought that, if we thought Jesus was washed up, there would be no point celebrating the passion. The loving compassion of God, the transcendent power of sacrifice and love, which is the inner story of the passion, does not allow us to think this.

A burden shared

It is true that Jesus is in a weakened state. But there is still a reservoir of strength to draw on. It is a strength that can be extended towards us. Carl Jung once said that only the wounded healer can heal. He was, of course, speaking about us. He was implying that only by an honest admission of our failures and failings can we make ourselves useful to others in distress. Jung was saying that the strong do not necessarily help the weak. We meet in common adversity. We share a brokenness. And in the sharing, in the commonality of pain and anguish, we both can move forward.

The tradition of Veronica and her cloth goes beyond the mere contact framed in the sixth station of the cross. At St Peter's in Rome there is a cloth that it has been claimed is the very one Veronica used. A devoted cult grew around this cloth and had its roots in this claim of authenticity. Yet there was more to it than that. It was no mere cloth. On it, embedded in it for all to see, was the very image of the Christ. His sweat and his blood had forged an imprinted likeness upon the cloth. We could see what Jesus looked like on the road to his death.

Now the vagaries of the cloth – its authenticity or otherwise – are, or should be to people of faith, irrelevant. The obsession with the relic, the issue of its authenticity, can too easily take us away from what is being extended to us in the contact with Veronica. Veronica steps forward to offer Jesus assistance. Yet he goes on to Golgotha to proclaim forgiveness to the world. The healer is wounded, but he heals universally through the ultimate wounding, death. The cross carried by the Christ is the symbol of both his execution and the liberating power of Jesus. That liberating power is available to everyone. It is there.

The name Veronica comes to us, some scholars say, because of this cloth. Now its truth or otherwise does not lie in the fabric but in the message of the sixth station. The name Veronica comes from two Greek words, *veron ikon*, which mean true image. The true image of the Christ, captured in story, in mythology, in what the Roman Catholic Church calls the Approved Cult, is not the mere piece of linen or whatever it was. The true image of Jesus Christ transcends this. It resides in the following simple statements. We can take ourselves completely to the Christ. We too can be healed. We too can have our sins forgiven. And in that, through and celebrating that, we can offer our lives back to Jesus.

Are we willing to stand out from the crowd for our faith? Are we prepared to do this, not from pride, but from our weakness? Can we reach out to the suffering Christ who holds the power to make us whole? In our reaching out, like the woman cured of bleeding, what secrets do we risk sharing? What in our lives needs healing? Is there a physical complaint we can offer to God? Do we harbour guilt for something we have done? Are we ashamed of thoughts? Do we regret something we have done? Are we honest in our relationships with God, ourselves, and others? The healing Christ can make us whole. All we have to do is be honest.

We should pause as we imagine Veronica. She leads us to more than a reflection of ourselves. She takes us into truth. The true image is really there. The true image is healing. It is a healing that is physical and spiritual. It is complete. It is marvellous. The true image is in that contact, be it a mere story, a myth or whatever: that Jesus, who will transcend his pain and torture, will offer us hope, love and forgiveness. There is an opportunity of healing for each and every one of us.

—— 3 ——

The women of Jerusalem

We are walking the way of the cross with women. We are
using their experiences – or what we imagine to have been
their experiences – to enable us to get closer to Jesus in
his final hours. We have seen that the forgiveness of Jesus
holds within it a challenge. It was a challenge to those
around him. In the same way it is a challenge for those
people who claim to be his followers. Are we prepared to
do as he does?

We have seen that the forgiveness of Jesus first involves
acceptance. In the first instance we have seen acceptance
by Jesus. We saw this particularly in the case of the gifts
offered by the woman with the alabaster jar. Then he
offers the gift of forgiveness. So we move to acceptance on
the part of the person to whom forgiveness is extended.

Jesus gives forgiveness freely. It is a gift. The recipient
accepts it. Likewise, we have seen comfort extended to
and by Jesus. This is illustrated by Veronica. While she
cannot heal, she can offer her sympathy and her compassion. She is able to give of her very self. She does this
through her actions towards the suffering Christ. Jesus
takes what she offers and gives in return. This is captured
in the myth of the image on the cloth. From this we learn

that we can echo her example by offering ourselves to Jesus.

In the first instance we do this through prayer. Prayer involves risk to feelings of our own self-sufficiency. In prayer we are challenged to acknowledge the reality of God. We can place everything – no matter how major or minuscule – before God. We can place before God our relationships with people around us. We also do it in action. We can be as Veronica. Our prayer and service to those around us can capture the imperative of Jesus's summary of the law.

> Jesus answered, 'The first is, "Hear O Israel: the Lord our God, the Lord is one; you shall love the Lord your God with all your heart, and with your all your soul, and with all your mind, and with all your strength." The second is this, "You shall love your neighbour as yourself." There is no other commandment greater than these.' (Mark 12.29–31)

Both prayer and service involve an exchange. In prayer we place ourselves before God and we await a response. There is no predicting what that response may be. Likewise, when we set out to give a practical or social expression to our faith, we cannot predetermine reaction to it. Those we are concerned with may not want our ministrations. They may even resent them. They can, and sometimes do, tell us they neither need nor care for charity.

No such rebuff is given by Jesus. When the women of the passion reach out to Jesus, the exchange happens. Jesus both receives and gives. The women also both give and receive. There is an exchange of gifts and sentiment.

Women by the wayside

In the next encounter Jesus has with women such a two-way exchange may not be immediately apparent. It runs the risk of being overwhelmed by grief. Such is the starkness of the incident in which women on the way come face to face with the suffering saviour. The poignancy of it should not be allowed to overpower an inherent challenge to their discipleship. Yet it is a firm warning that there is a cost in discipleship.

> A great number of the people followed him, and among them were women who were beating their breasts and wailing for him. (Luke 23.27)

In one translation of the Bible this verse is rendered along the lines that people were following and, almost as an afterthought, that there were also women. If one were to read this translation on its own, what we do assume is the meaning the evangelist is trying to give? Could it be that women are not people? The answer has to be an emphatic no. It is true that the way numbers are accounted for in the gospels can be a mite confusing. The collective noun 'people' might sometimes be thought to exclude women. But at other times it is clearer. In the feeding of the five thousand, after the five loaves and two fish have been blessed, broken and distributed, Matthew tells us:

> And those who ate were about five thousand men, besides women and children. (Matthew 14.21)

So the feeding of the five thousand, taking into account the 'besides' mentioned in that text, means that it was actually the feeding of who knows how many. The same applies to the feeding of the four thousand. On this occasion seven loaves are mentioned, as well as a few small fish. Jesus gives thanks, breaks them, gives them to the disciples to distribute to the crowds.

> And all of them ate and were filled; and they took the broken pieces left over, seven baskets full. Those who had eaten were four thousand men, besides women and children. (Matthew 15.37–8)

We have to be careful here. It might again be construed, from our modern standpoint, that the women are being discounted. Actually it is not the case. Far from being marginalized, women are shown as being fully recognized in the presence of Jesus. Women were fully accepted as followers. Some were more than mere followers, and were instrumental in maintaining Jesus and fellow disciples as the Lord went about in his active ministry. To some extent Jesus relied on women to keep his retinue in food, accommodation and clothing.

> Soon afterwards he went on through cities and villages, proclaiming and bringing the good news of the kingdom of God. The twelve were with him, as well as some women who had been cured of evil spirits and infirmities: Mary, called Magdalene, from whom seven demons had gone out, and Joanna, the wife of Herod's steward Chuza, and Susanna, and many others who provided for them out of their own resources. (Luke 8.1–3)

The women, as far as we can tell, were independent. They had access to their own means. That is made very clear. Jesus accepted the women as followers. He accepted the care they provided, which extended beyond the person of Jesus himself to include other disciples.

This independence is borne out in the passion. We are told in the Gospels of Matthew and Mark that women were present as Jesus was dying. At his execution some were looking on. It is more than a suggestion that even females were allowed to watch the horrors of crucifixion. It alerts us to their full witnessing of the life and death of the Christ. To underscore this there is specific mention of these women at Golgotha. We are told who some of them were. They are named. They are Mary Magdalene, Mary the mother of James and Joseph, the mother of the sons of Zebedee. Salome is mentioned in the Gospel of Mark only. In all, however, we are told that there were many others.

But we are running slightly ahead of ourselves. Golgotha lies at the end of the Via Dolorosa.

On his way to the Place of the Skull there is another encounter between Jesus and women. It is enshrined in both Scripture and in the stations of the cross. It occurs as Jesus struggles with the cross. The women involved are local residents. They are described as such. The name of their home town has become part of their identification. They are the women of Jerusalem. As far as we know, because it is not explicitly mentioned either way in the gospels, they are not part of his retinue. The surprising thing is that it is Jesus who takes the initiative. Luke's Gospel mentions that they are following and are beating their breasts and wailing.

But Jesus turned to them and said, 'Daughters of Jerusalem, do not weep for me, but weep for yourselves and for your children. For the days are surely coming when they will say, "Blessed are the barren, and the wombs that never bore, and the breasts that never nursed." Then they will begin to say to the mountains, "Fall on us"; and to the hills, "Cover us". For if they do this when the wood is green, what will happen when it is dry?' (Luke 23.28–31)

If you were making the stations of the cross, this would be the eighth station. The representation of this encounter is splendidly captured in many renderings of the scene. The artist can draw on a wide range of emotions. Jesus, weighed down by the cross, is speaking with the women. The crowd gawps. Guards look on in a mixture of suspicion and puzzlement. Some of the women look straight at Jesus. One may be reaching out her hand. Some are turning their faces from the scene. There is sometimes active weeping and wailing. Such a display is a physical expression of inner pain. Pain is being vented publicly. It is not being bottled up.

A grieving community

We have a great deal to learn from the way other cultures deal with death. In Britain, despite the public displays of grief following the death of Diana, Princess of Wales, mourning is still relatively restrained and private. This is far from what is considered normal in the Middle East, where some customs surrounding death have a long tradition. There we can see a very public aspect of grief.

Nowhere is this more evident than in the gospels. When Jesus is called to go to the aid of the daughter of Jairus, the community is already gathered. Jairus tells Jesus that the child is at the point of death. Yet when he arrives at the home he is told he is too late.

When they came to the house of the leader of the

synagogue, he saw a commotion, people weeping and wailing loudly. (Mark 5.38)

There is nothing forced or unnatural in this. When Jesus suggests that the child is sleeping the response is equally unrestrained. He is met with derision. The people laugh at him. Yet he surprises everyone, even those who do not want to trouble the Christ further, by bringing the girl back to life. What makes this miracle all the more intriguing is the lack of a detailed reported response of those present. After she gets up it becomes a surprisingly low key and practical affair.

At this they were overcome with amazement. He strictly ordered them that no one should know this, and told them to give her something to eat. (Mark 5.42–3)

A similar public outburst of grief is reported by John when he writes of the death of Lazarus. Jesus goes to Bethany, but only after waiting to make sure Lazarus is well and truly dead. He has a purpose in mind.

Then Jesus told them plainly, 'Lazarus is dead. For your sake, I am glad that I was not there, so that you may believe. But let us go to him.' (John 11.14–15)

As Jesus is on the way, Martha, Lazarus's sister, gets up and goes to meet him. Her sister Mary hears this and she too goes to meet Jesus.

Now Jesus had not yet come to the village, but was still at the place where Martha had met him. The Jews who were with her in the house, consoling her, saw Mary get up quickly and go out. They followed her because they thought she was going to the tomb to weep there. (John 11.30–1)

Such is the public nature of the mourning. People think she is going to continue her lamentation at her brother's grave. So that she will not do this alone they go with her. When she does not do what they expected they still accompany her. It is their social duty to be with her. Mary goes to meet Jesus. She kneels at his feet and says:

'Lord, if you had been here, my brother would not have died.' (John 11.32)

The Christ's response is prefaced by a reminder to the reader that this was not a private matter.

When Jesus saw her weeping, and the Jews who were with her also weeping, he was greatly disturbed in spirit and deeply moved. (John 11.33)

It is worth noting the reaction of Jesus. He is greatly disturbed in spirit. He is deeply moved. This is more than a slight feeling of empathy. It is certainly not discomfort in the face of another's suffering. It is an open profession of grief. He makes no attempt to shield others from his feelings. What occurs is a public display by Jesus of his feelings for all to see.

He said, 'Where have you laid him?' They said to him, 'Lord, come and see.' Jesus began to weep. So the Jews said, 'See how he loved him!' (John 11.34–6)

Jesus shares with them a universal reaction to death. The death of a loved one is painful. An exchange ensues because of Jesus's letting others see his emotions. He can share his pain with Martha and Mary and those who are with them. And they can share in his grief. This is an individual experience for each person, yet the emotion can encompass all in its common expression.

Being a disciple does not bring an exemption from the difficulties. Lazarus, a disciple and a friend, was not spared death. Even after having been raised from the dead, he still heads for a second death. He, along with his sisters and other followers of Jesus, does not evade sickness, pain or death. Discipleship means engagement with the world, not as we would have it, but as it is. It involves grief, a grief shared by the Christ.

You may have seen on the television news reports of funerals in the Middle East. Often there is a great outpouring of pain. Sometimes this is inextricably linked with anger. The event in which an individual dies can trigger and be a focus of this emotional outcry. Political killings can cause rage. Ongoing oppression can inspire as much as it can lead to feelings of impotence. All these can be expressed at funeral processions or when a body is laid to rest. When we watch at a geographical, political and cultural remove, the causes may be lost on us. But what we see has the same manifestation. We witness public distress.

In some cultures there are full-time, though one would hesitate to call them professional, weepers and wailers. Those of cynical bent could say that this is only show. They will discount it as sham. But it also represents a deep cultural expression, a liturgical manifestation if you like, of how those affected by a loss are feeling. In grief we are often attempting to remain in control. We are trying to rein in a complex mixture of feelings that may include loss, anger and guilt. But the weepers and wailers can release it for us. They, like a choir singing parts of a service on behalf of the congregation, can, if they do it properly, give voice to the mute songs of our hearts.

As the women of Jerusalem encounter Jesus, let us consider both sides of that conundrum. That is, that the women may be public agents of someone else's private grief. They are doing the community's work. Or perhaps they are truly expressing their own personal pain. Either way, the encounter can inform us of the cost involved in making a commitment to Jesus.

A private pain

Let us look first at personal pain. Real grief is being displayed in public. The women are so moved by this man's situation that they cry. It must be remembered that crucifixions had happened before in Jerusalem. Jesus is not the first man to walk these streets to his death. In fact, crucifixion was a relatively common method of execution used by the occupying Roman power. The women's distress has a more individual quality. They are particularly overcome with pity at the brutality being meted out on a particular man. They are lamenting what is happening to Jesus. They are, however, powerless to put a stop to it. They are all too aware of this. They cannot change what Pilate has commanded his soldiers to carry out. They are no more able to alter the course of events than was Pontius Pilate's wife. She attempted and failed in her intervention to counter the events set in train by her husband. She had had a dream.

> While he was sitting on the judgement seat, his wife sent word to him, 'Have nothing to do with that innocent man, for today I have suffered a great deal because of a dream about him.' (Matthew 27.19)

Pilate's wife suffers. This is ripe for rumination. What was it that gave rise to her disquiet? For all we know, she had never met Jesus. To what extent she knew of him, his teaching or the miracles he wrought, is speculative. Yet in the passion of Jesus, it is the wife of Pilate who suffers. Perhaps she does so because she knows what fate has in store for someone condemned to death on the cross. It may be she sympathizes with the Christ, recognizing, as Pilate himself has told the crowds, that the accused man is innocent. Or could she have had a premonition of how history would treat her husband? Did she know that taunts would be made up of his name? That the name 'Pontius Pilate' would become an epithet equivalent to 'Traitor!'?

When Jesus meets the women of Jerusalem the court of Pilate is far behind. It has been left at the bottom of the hill. The stations of the cross use the condemnation to death for the first meditation. A great deal has happened since then. We are now some way up the Via Dolorosa.

The women of Jerusalem meet Jesus in the depths of their own despair. They are moved by the plight of the suffering man before them. They are absorbed in his pain and distressed by their inability to alter his fate. But there may be even more personal factors that could augment their anguish. What if these women are more than mere residents of Jerusalem witnessing an event over which they have no control?

Let us consider the possibility of their being more than mere followers of Jesus. They may not be of that exalted inner circle, those women who were ministering to Jesus, but they could be his disciples. Their discipleship could range from the casual to those who have a precise personal connection with him. Perhaps one of their number had been the beneficiary of the healing ministry of Jesus. One of them may have been cured physically. Let us suppose one is the same nameless woman who has been suggested for Veronica. This is the woman who was healed as Jesus made his way to see if he could cure the ailing daughter of Jairus.

Crowds were pressing in on Jesus. He feels some of his power leave him. A woman who has been bleeding for twelve years has made her way through the crowds. She believes that if she only touches his clothes she will be healed. She is rewarded with a physical cure. Jesus tells her, after she has come forward in fear and trembling, that her faith has been rewarded.

Nor did Jesus restrict his healings to those who were ill. We have seen in the case of Lazarus that Jesus himself could be moved by the scenes of pain and grief he witnessed. His healings did and do transcend death. This can be seen in an incident in which Jesus and his followers become involved almost by chance.

> Soon afterwards he went to a town called Nain, and his disciples and a large crowd went with him. As he approached the gate of the town, a man who had died was being carried out. He was his mother's only son, and she was a widow; and with her was a large crowd from the town. (Luke 7.11–12)

There is no appeal to Jesus. The grieving mother does not ask for his help. It seems unlikely that she even knew who he was. Neither the crowds nor the disciples press Jesus to use his healing powers. It is a more instinctive and immediate reaction.

> When the Lord saw her, he had compassion for her and said to her, 'Do not weep.' (Luke 7.13)

Interestingly, this is the same advice he offers to the weeping and wailing women of Jerusalem as he is on the road to his own death. Yet Jesus does not restrict himself to a command that the tears should stop.

> Then he came forward and touched the bier, and the bearers stood still. And he said, 'Young man, I say to you, rise!' The dead man sat up and began to speak, and Jesus gave him to his mother. (Luke 7.14–15)

The healings of Jesus transcended physical cures. It has been pointed out often, and for good reason, that Jesus's healing gifts were of benefit to the whole person. He was a holistic healer. He treated the complete being. This was because he could see into people and locate that part that was out of kilter with the physical or spiritual harmony we all aspire to. Jesus knew wholeness and could offer it to others. One way he did this was through the forgiveness of sins. The saying for which he was reviled time and time again was as simple as it was devastating to those who heard it. 'Your sins are forgiven', he would say. This led to repeated accusations of blasphemy against Jesus.

Imagine one of the women of Jerusalem as the beneficiary of this forgiveness. In the first chapter, we spent some time looking at the woman with the alabaster jar. In Luke's account of this encounter, much is made of the common knowledge of the woman's sinfulness. One guest says that if Jesus were the prophet others claim him to be, he would know what sort of woman was weeping over his feet. The truth is that he does know. And it is because he knows precisely what she is that he can offer wholeness rather than condemnation. He frees her from her past to allow her present to become a liberation. This liberation is the start of a new life.

Then he said to her, 'Your sins are forgiven.' But those

who were at the table with him began to say to themselves, 'Who is this who even forgives sins?' And he said to the woman, 'Your faith has saved you; go in peace.' (Luke 7.48–50)

For us there is an even broader effect. The healing of one of the members of the Church should be seen in terms of the corporate recovery of health. The healing power of Jesus is not confined to an individual but, if we take discipleship seriously, extends to the whole body of believers. To that end, there can be no room for petty jealousy within our ranks. Where healing appears in one disciple's life, the Church should rejoice because it too experiences the cure.

Perhaps one of the weeping women on the road to Golgotha is the woman with the alabaster jar. Touched by the healing hand or spirit of Jesus, she laments that she cannot extend to him even part of what he extended to her. She is powerless, impotent in the face of his suffering.

A public pain

The second facet of the women's weeping to ponder is a public one. Let us imagine that these women of Jerusalem are a group of weepers and wailers. We have already considered some aspects of this public function in the context of the Christ's healing ministry. By doing so, we recognize that a public display of grief is not necessarily done to indulge what could be seen as hysterical or histrionic tendencies. Rather, it too is a method of healing. It allows those involved a freedom to join in. Or if one is not ready to do so, it ensures that some of the pent up pain and anguish is aired on their behalf. Perhaps a group of such women acted on behalf of the Jewish people to add emotional gravitas to the processions of condemned men in the city. The judicial process has ensured that the death of Jesus will be at the hands of the Roman hierarchy. Now it is only appropriate that the local population behave in a seemly manner.

Whatever the reason for their presence, Jesus notices them. He responds to them. Indeed, he takes the initiative. By speaking to the women, Jesus acts as he has before. And what he says is in keeping with what has been in evidence throughout his ministry. Women are welcome. He has said that all along. Women could sit with him. They could hear his teaching. But here, in their grief and despair, Jesus implores them to think of the realities of their situation. He tells them to weep for themselves and for their children.

This is a startling thing to say. Jesus inverts the situation. Weighed down by the cross, Jesus attempts to lift a burden from the women. He personalizes their public function. He connects their inner lives to the public manifestation of grief. He makes them whole.

Be it a personal grief or a public responsibility, Jesus suggests the women's actions are misplaced. This is not the first time Jesus has turned a situation on its head. Such events happened often while he taught. One incident involves a woman who calls from the crowd.

While he was saying this, a woman in the crowd raised her voice and said to him, 'Blessed is the womb that bore you and the breasts that nursed you!' But he said, 'Blessed rather are those who hear the word of God and obey it!' (Luke 11.27–8)

Jesus shifts the focus from what is said to what it

63

implies. He turns the subject from his mother to the issue behind the woman's comment. By doing this, the woman and those around her are urged to consider their own lives. This is a subversive way of teaching. Rather than bask in the reflected glory of the comment about his mother – Mary is praised because of her son – Jesus wants all to think about what they hear and how they live. He wants people to take on board what he is saying. Jesus wants them to listen to the word of God and urges them to act on it. Moreover, he wants them to obey it.

Time and time again Jesus does this. People ask him questions and he shoots through the camouflage of the query to the heart of the person asking it. His response is often a personal challenge. Perhaps the most famous example of this is Jesus's encounter with the rich young man. He has approached Jesus for encouragement. He is seeking endorsement for his life and his actions. Yet Jesus, in a compassionate confrontation, makes the young man question his very self.

The episode involves a range of inversions and contradictions. The man begins by kneeling in front of Jesus. In spite of the inferior posture, the young man wants affirmation of his current way of life. If he secures it he can take solace in the thought that he has done enough. Despite asking what he needs for eternal life, he is seeking approval. He wants to be told he is well on the way. But Jesus, after going through the law, looks on him sympathetically.

> Jesus, looking at him, loved him and said, 'You lack one thing; go, sell what you own, and give the money to the poor, and you will have treasure in heaven; then come, follow me.' (Mark 10.21)

Such sympathy is too much for the rich young man. It is not what he was after. Jesus's call goes to the very nub of his life. Jesus's cure for the young man is too radical, too thoroughgoing for him. He is seeking comfort for himself. But Jesus wants his followers to go beyond personal comfort. He wants them to challenge themselves to show forth the love of God in their own lives and to join others. The personal must be married to the corporate.

> When he heard this, he was shocked and went away grieving, for he had many possessions. (Mark 10.22)

Jesus had the talent to see into the core of a person's being. Those who came to him did not always get what they wanted. The power of the Christ saw through the dross to the real issue. Because he was able to identify what was wrong, what was incomplete in the lives of those who came to him, it is not surprising that he could make them whole. He did this in many ways – by healing, curing, in forgiveness, rebuke or challenge. He sees into the person and responds in a way appropriate to that person's needs.

This what Jesus does in the face of the grief of the women of Jerusalem. Even if these women were full-time weepers and wailers, Jesus still offers them such a challenge. The display, as far as he is concerned, is misplaced. There is no need for it, because there is something greater to come. Public displays, whatever their nature, will be futile.

> 'Then they will begin to say to the mountains, "Fall on us" and to the hills, "Cover us". For if they do this when the wood is green, what will happen when it is dry?' (Luke 23.30–1)

65

The cost of discipleship

In this encounter the women of Jerusalem are being challenged. The man who is being mourned continues in his
prophetic role. His words are not a hollow kind of reas-
surance, a phatic kind of 'There, there.' No, even on the
road to his death, he does not drop his prophetic nature.
He is saying to them, 'See through this'. He wants them to
put to one side their feelings or the public show of them
and look to what is at stake. He is telling them to look
beyond the suffering. He wants them, as he wants each
and every one of us, to see where this suffering may lead.
He wants them to look to the Lord.

In this encounter Jesus gives us the challenge of following him. Possible comfort is eclipsed. His words to the
women quickly move from sympathy for individuals to
the consequence for the broader community. This is not a
healing like that extended to the woman with the issue of
blood. This is not comfort like the forgiveness of sins of
the woman with the alabaster jar when she anointed him.
This is the Jesus who challenged those who met him to see
what is at stake. He makes them see how their individual
and community lives must be confronted.

We know that Jesus will move to his death where he will
offer himself as a sacrifice for all people and for all time.
We know that Jesus will take upon himself all our guilt,
our failings and our sin. In doing this we meet him. We
meet him, as the women of Jerusalem did, on the road to
Golgotha. And he looks at us and sees what is lacking in
our lives. This God made man can discern that part of us
that needs healing. He knows how to make us whole. And
he offers himself as the cure. In his death the world will be
reconciled to God. By God's self-offering at Calvary, the

world can move closer to God. That is the place to which the Christ is leading us. At the same time, he halts on the way. In that hiatus, he challenges us. He challenges us as he did the rich young man to consider for ourselves what it is that is preventing our cure. The Lord says to us, 'Think! Act!' This is the broken, suffering Lord who will transform the darkness of our lives into light. He says, 'Come, follow me', even as he staggers towards his liberating death.

4

Mary, the mother of Jesus

In any consideration of women of the passion it is impossible to avoid Mary, the mother of Jesus. She moves from her central place in God's action of the incarnation to become a prime witness in the redemption achieved by the death of the child she bore.

Over the years a lot of activity and anger has been generated around Mary. Such anger has taken many forms. Much early feminist thinking was critical of the way Mary was held up as particular role model for women. Her critics said Mary was far from being a person to aspire to. Rather, Mary was oppressive. Her popular image was thought to restrict the scope of women's talents and ambitions. Women had been told to accept their lot. This meant their future could be played out in a limited way. They had two options. They were confined to pious virginity or to servile childbearing and drudgery in the home. Pious virginity had its expression in the cloister or in the spectre of spinster aunts. This, of course, puts to one side why women who stayed single in the community or joined the communal life of the convent were considered of lesser worth. Attacks were often couched in terms of these women not fulfilling their potential as sexual beings.

Such thought likewise condemned those who chose to see motherhood as a full-time vocation.

Whatever the root cause for these attacks, the mother of Jesus was often held personally responsible for contributing to the suppression of women. Discussion was complicated by the absence of reliable information about the home life of Mary and Joseph in Nazareth. It was thought this lack of knowledge was overcompensated for by anti-women romantic notions compounded by plain fear and distrust.

It is not just secular feminism that has been critical of the Blessed Virgin Mary. Within the Church itself the mother of Jesus has been the catalyst for much bitterness and many battles. Claims and counterclaims about her role within the public and devotional life of the Church have been made for centuries. They continue to be made today. These debates often centre on what, if any, place she should play in prayer and liturgy. To see such antithesis as the divide between protestant and catholic theology is, despite its initial attraction, too simplistic. As is often the case in these debates, the details are much more interesting and revealing than such broad descriptive polarities allow.

Yet much of the criticism between these extremes has its focus in the mother of the Christ. It has to be admitted that much of it is deserved. But it must also be acknowledged that the bulk of the criticism was not really of the Blessed Virgin Mary herself. The causes for complaint were mostly based on the myths and cults that have grown up around her. Several works have sought to debunk these myths. Some have a distinctly polemic nature. The authors set out to demolish the superstitions and excesses of Marian devotion. However, one writer, John Macquarrie, has done so with the aim of trying to make

70

Mary a person and saint who has relevance for all Christians.

In this chapter we shall consider Mary and what we might be able to infer from her contacts with her son during his last hours. We will do this in the spirit advocated by John Macquarrie. This is not to add to the myths and cults but to attempt to see what we can understand or imagine from Mary's walk along the Via Dolorosa. By doing that, we may come closer to understanding why Mary does hold so important a place in the life, heritage and practice of the Church.

Hail Mary

First and foremost has to be Mary's unique position among all people in the gospels. It is Mary who sees the entire Jesus story through from prediction to accomplishment. It was to a young woman in Nazareth that God sent the angel Gabriel. Mary was the person to whom God spoke, through Gabriel, saying that she would bear a child who would become great and holy. The account of the annunciation in Luke is what forms the basis for the prayer, the Hail Mary, widely used and greatly loved by many in the broader Church. The first half of the prayer has a solid biblical base. Gabriel appears to Mary.

And he came to her and said, 'Greetings, favoured one! The Lord is with you.' (Luke 1.28)

This salutation is combined with another. The second greeting comes from her cousin, the once barren Elizabeth, when the likewise pregnant Mary visits her in a Judean town in the hill country.

71

And Elizabeth was filled with the Holy Spirit and exclaimed with a loud cry, 'Blessed are you among women, and blessed is the fruit of your womb.' (Luke 1.41–2)

Mary was the woman delivered of a baby boy in Bethlehem when there was no room at the inn. The Virgin Mary is reported in the gospels to have seen this boy grow in strength and wisdom. When we read the one incident of his childhood recorded in Scripture we might even say Jesus had grown to precocious knowledge. This is when Jesus went missing at the age of twelve after a journey to Jerusalem. The surprise of his parents at his being found in the temple after three days, sitting among the teachers and asking questions, is real enough.

When his parents saw him they were astonished; and his mother said to him, 'Child, why have you treated us like this? Look, your father and I have been searching for you in great anxiety.' (Luke 2.48)

The Virgin Mary saw Jesus go about in his active ministry. The gospels tell us that. We are told in John's Gospel that the Virgin Mary was present when Jesus performed his first sign. She was more than a mere spectator. She was instrumental in his action of turning water into wine at the wedding at Cana. She is rebuked by him for telling him the wine has run out.

And Jesus said to her, 'Woman, what concern is that to you or to me? My hour has not yet come.' (John 2.4)

Despite this, she tells the servants to follow his instructions. And the first sign recorded in John's Gospel is performed. This is one of many incidents in Scripture where she is mentioned as being with or following her son. She suffers another rebuke when she visits Jesus with members of the family.

> While he was still speaking to the crowds, his mother and his brothers were standing outside, wanting to speak to him. Someone told him, 'Look, your mother and your brothers are standing outside, wanting to speak to you.' But to the one who had told him this, Jesus replied, 'Who is my mother, and who are my brothers?' And pointing to his disciples, he said, 'Here are my mother and my brothers! For whoever does the will of my Father in heaven is my brother and sister and mother.' (Matthew 12.46–50)

Mary's life is an important one because of all these events. She is a witness repeatedly alluded to in the gospels. And this witness is of itself a compelling reason to think of Mary when we consider the way of the cross. The Virgin Mary was there. She was a suffering witness to the pain that liberates the world. These sufferings are captured in one of the many titles she has gained over the years – Mary, Queen of Sorrows. These sorrows are sometimes the cause for her critics' complaints. It has to be conceded that some versions of the stations of the cross can seem like the stations of Mary. Indeed, a number of versions are almost exclusively a meditation of her plight. Each meditative station is followed by prayers to or about her. The authors of such manuals have no qualms about this, often calling the meditations 'Mary's Way Of The Cross'. This might be excessive.

Blessed art thou among women

Yet to think of Mary in relation to the passion is understandable. There is some compelling evidence to do so, and one undeniable link: she was there – Mary was present at the death of her first-born son. The mother stood at the foot of the cross as her child died in the horrifying gore of crucifixion. The gospels tell us that too.

Is it any wonder, then, that the Blessed Virgin Mary is so important to the Church? When we remember the actual scope of her experience as reported in Scripture we cannot ignore her. The passion of Jesus has a human quality seen through the sufferings of Mary. The passion compels us to think of her. It is for that reason, and for the added value given to her experience by our imagination, that we can learn from Mary. We can try to empathize with her. We can attempt to share her joys and suffering.

Prayer is a legitimate way of trying to deepen our understanding of events recorded in Scripture. This is one of the great gifts of contemplation. We shall meditate upon Mary's contacts with Jesus in his final hours. These events can move us. We can wonder at the ordinary and extraordinary tragedy involved in the last day of her son's life. We may marvel at her resilience and endurance.

Much of what we have to think about is painful. Much of it we might prefer to avoid. But the passion makes up a substantial part of the gospels. Good Friday is the day the Church remembers the reality of the death of Jesus Christ. It is true that we know this brutal end has ramifications for us. We are saved by it. We are freed from our sins by it. But we also must acknowledge that this was no easy task. In fact, the sufferings that can so distress and unsettle us were predicted to the Blessed Virgin Mary.

Remember when Jesus was brought into the temple as a baby. As laid down by the Mosaic law, Mary came to the temple to be declared ritually clean after childbirth. She, in the company of her husband Joseph, came to the temple for purification. They brought with them the prescribed sacrifice of two turtle doves or young pigeons. It was also the occasion of dedicating their first-born son to the Lord. In the process of doing so, Jesus is acclaimed by a woman and a man. Luke records her identity in some detail.

There was also a prophet, Anna the daughter of Phanuel, of the tribe of Asher. She was of a great age, having lived with her husband seven years after her marriage, then as a widow to the age of eighty-four. (Luke 2.36–7)

Her devotion to God is attested to. Indeed, she has given her life to the Lord.

She never left the temple but worshipped there with fasting and prayer night and day. (Luke 2.37)

Yet it is not who Anna is that is of overriding importance. It is what she says and about whom she says it. She is in the temple as Mary and Joseph present Jesus to the righteous man, Simeon.

At that moment she came, and began to praise God and speak about the child to all who were looking for the redemption of Jerusalem. (Luke 2.38)

By her public declaration, Anna complements and augments what Simeon says when he sees the boy. Simeon declares Jesus to be the one who is awaited. This child will redeem both non-Jew and Jew alike.

And the child's father and mother were amazed at what was being said about him. Then Simeon blessed them and said to his mother Mary, 'This child is destined for the falling and the rising of many in Israel, and to be a sign that will be opposed, so that the inner thoughts of many will be revealed – and a sword will pierce your own soul too.' (Luke 2.33–5)

It is this sword piercing the soul of Mary that cannot be discounted. Our consideration of the Virgin Mary in her son's final hours must be piercing. It is an uncomfortable, at times harrowing, reality that the passion narratives tell. Mary figures three times. These are captured in the stations of the cross.

The first contact between Jesus and Mary is in the fourth station of the cross, usually simply entitled Jesus Meets His Mother. It is a poignant meditation. It is one where we can consider some of the agony both must have been in. This is a shared agony because the passion of Jesus was not easy for him. Some have argued that, as God, Jesus was not subject to the trials of human experience. They claim that the suffering and pain of Jesus was apparently human but, because he was God, not really so. The Church has rejected such notions. It is contrary to the profession of the faith encapsulated in the credal formulae. Jesus was truly God and truly man.

Madonna and child

By the fourth station Jesus has been subjected to a range of indignities. His clothes have been taken from him. He has been dressed up in a purple robe. A crown of thorns has been placed on his head. Thus attired, the soldiers have mocked him. He has been physically tortured. The gospels record variously that he was scourged, spat upon and beaten. Scourging was an especially barbaric form of maltreatment. The ends of the leather thongs would have been tipped with sharp edges such as pieces of metal or bone. Any lashing would be calculated to cut the skin. The pain of the whipping is intensified because of the cruelty involved. It would enervate its victims. Many of them would pass out. Some are reported to have died.

Having coped with these abuses, Jesus has taken the weight of the cross and struggled on the road to Golgotha. The stations of the cross provide opportunities to focus on the pain of his load by having Jesus fall three times. By the time he meets his mother on the Via Dolorosa, he has tripped and fallen once.

Mary looks at her son with a profound pity. Yet she is also aware of her impotence to intervene in the events that will lead to his death. Mary, like most of the people on the Via Dolorosa, would know what end Jesus was to meet. Crucifixion was a public method of execution, and the processions to the place of death were not uncommon.

Jesus looks at his mother knowing he can say nothing to ease her anguish. He himself is wracked by pain. His body throbs with bruising and lacerations. He is hot, uncomfortable and distressed. Neither mother nor son can offer much solace to the other. There is a shared resignation to what is occurring.

The predictions of Simeon and Anna come to the fore. Anna's foretelling of Jerusalem's redemption is not without physical and emotional cost. Often, when pausing at the fourth station of the cross, Simeon's words are called to mind. Sometimes the text involving the sword piercing Mary's heart is quoted. This can heighten the effect of what the artist has provided visually. In a set of line drawings by the artist Brandy Pearson the scene of the fourth station is rendered without people. She has simply chosen to draw a heart skewered on a sword. Painful as it may be, the fourth station is a silent precursor to what is to follow.

In some other newer settings of the stations, in line with the ongoing revisionism the Church is not immune from, some artists have added two more stations. The new stations are based on incidents recorded in Scripture. These might be preferred by some people to the usual stations, which are merely based on pious traditions. The first of these two new inclusions is Jesus talking to his mother and John the apostle. The second is the deposition, that moment when the body of Jesus is taken down from the cross.

Let us first concentrate on the biblical station of her contact with her son as he hangs dying. In this encounter she stands there, helpless, at the foot of the cross. It is all the more harrowing because of what had been predicted all those years before. We can assume that all Mary may have feared has now come true. The first thing to note is that Mary is not alone. The community of Jesus's followers is with her. Just how this occurs varies in the gospels. In the events recorded in the synoptic gospels other women are on hand to watch Jesus die. These women watch from afar. We have considered and will consider them in the chapters on the women of Jerusalem and Mary Magdalene respectively. The Gospel of John bears similar witness. We are informed that women are there. They include some of the same women Mark and Matthew place at a distance. The community is made up of Mary the mother of the Christ, these women and the disciple whom Jesus loved. It is to Mary and John that Jesus speaks. Through John, therefore, we can join Mary at the foot of the cross.

Christians cherish the cross because we are freed by it. This is one of those subversive aspects that make the Christian faith what it is. A group of people wear the image of an instrument of torture to proclaim their faith. Sometimes it is sported as mere ornamental jewellery. But for those who believe, the cross is a profound symbol. It speaks of faith in the one who hung on it. And it is a faith in what was achieved by his doing so. As it says in the first epistle of Peter:

He himself bore our sins in his body on the cross, so that, free from sins, we might live for righteousness; by his wounds you have been healed. For you were going astray like sheep, but now you have returned to the shepherd and guardian of your souls. (1 Peter 2.24–5)

Peter points to the dual benefits of the cross. First, there is the personal. And the second is communal. The cross is a sign of liberation for individuals and the world as a whole. It has secondary power for us when we consider when Jesus warned his disciples what following him would involve.

Then he said to them all, 'If any want to become my followers, let them deny themselves and take up their cross daily and follow me. For those who want to save their life will lose it, and those who lose their life for my sake will save it.' (Luke 9.23–4)

What is important to remember is that each person has an individual cross. Some translations of the Bible can cause confusion on this point. It is clear that Jesus was warning the disciples then, as he warns us now, that it is not his cross that we have to bear. It is our own. Each and every one of us has a cross to bear. And it is appropriate to us, our time, and our culture. It is personal. In bearing one's own cross, Jesus draws us into a personal relationship. The cost of that relationship is great. It draws us into a broader group. So what begins as an individual relationship is widened to a community. Subversion of traditional values continues inside the Christian society.

'Whoever loves father or mother more than me is not worthy of me; and whoever does not take up the cross and follow me is not worthy of me.' (Matthew 10.38)

It is a stern warning. Our discipleship, our ongoing preparedness to deal with our circumstances, is what determines our worthiness. So how we follow the Christ is up to us. There is not a set pattern. Each and every life can be used by and for God. Each and every life can be absorbed into the Christian community.

Mary, the mother of Jesus, was not carrying the cross of her son. She could not. She was not the teacher who so angered the authorities. She was not the worker of miracles. She was not the one who attracted the masses. She was not arrested and put on trial. Her cross was to follow her son, literally if we take the fourth station as an incident quite early on the road to Golgotha, on the way to his death.

At the hour of death

This retracing of the steps of her condemned son has a power for us too. Through Mary we can see both the fulfilment of prophecy and the desperate disappointment of watching a young man die. This resignation is poignant. Some anti-Marian criticism is based on what is viewed as the over-romanticized action of Mary saying yes to God's will at the annunciation. Yet that acceptance of her fate is worth putting into context. Not only did Mary accept the will of God in bearing Jesus. She also had to deal with the end of her son's life. In the execution of Jesus we can see the evaporation of the best efforts of parents, family and friends. These people have tried to give the best to the boy now a man. And all those efforts seem to be sacrificed with him as he dies on the cross.

Death by crucifixion could never be described – as if any method of execution could – as humane. It was long, drawn out and grisly. Men were hauled aloft. Their energy was sapped as they tried to hold themselves straight. Their joints were under stress. Their muscles were aching and, in the end, they collapsed. There was strain on the heart, lungs, bones and muscles. Think for a moment of the effect all this physical pain could have in the mind. This is far beyond mere headache. Your mind is battling with the confused distress of trying to hold yourself together, knowing that every effort to get you to this place has had but one aim, and that is to see you dead.

There would be a range of reactions in the people at Golgotha to what was going on. But what of Mary? She stood there as a witness to see her child die. Many have tried imaginatively to place themselves at the foot of the cross. The words of the *Stabat Mater*, set to music by composers ranging from Palestrina to Rossini, are often used for this purpose. Yet they can fall short of the bleakness involved. They merely urge us to empathize with Mary. They do not attempt to give us an insight into her thoughts. What memories can offer her comfort? We have already visited Jesus's birth, the predictions in the temple, the sole incident of his childhood recorded in Scripture, Mary's presence at his teaching. There is a wealth of human experience left unrecorded. These include conversations ranging from the petty to the profound. Or perhaps there is a treasured moment when the young boy shared something with her. There are many personal insights in each life, privately treasured by those near and dear. But would she even be able to distract herself with them?

To see someone you love die can be deeply moving. Many people speak of the impact of being with a loved one during their final hours. Having been present at the death, they know what their loved one experienced. If someone has been ill for years, praying with them can be a powerful witness to life. Just being there can be a testament to hope. Such a vigil can also be kept out of respect. It can also provide comfort for those who mourn. When we read the Bible we can see that gathering for the death of someone was considered culturally appropriate. In many cultures it is still done today. When the last breaths are anticipated the family gathers. Perhaps a priest is called. The wider community is there, prayerfully in distress, for the dying person and for each other.

Jesus was not a sick man. He was not some ancient come to the end of his days with the devoted clan around his bed. People, by and large, were not there out of respect. We have already suggested that they were there for several reasons. These ranged from professional duty on the part of the soldiers to the relishing of the gory spectacle for others. Some, however, were there out of grief and compassion. And some of these people were close by.

Meanwhile, standing near the cross of Jesus were his mother, and his mother's sister, Mary the wife of Clopas, and Mary Magdalene. When Jesus saw his mother and the disciple he loved standing beside her, he said to his mother, 'Woman, here is your son.' Then he said to the disciple, 'Here is your mother.' And from that hour the disciple took her into his own home. (John 19.25–7)

This is an extraordinary incident. It is often skipped over because of the compelling nature of the narrative. Yet it is worth spending time on. In it the roles of parent and child are reversed. Mary is helpless. The woman who gave birth to a boy, who suckled and cared for him, can do nothing. She was involved in his education and development. She saw him become the teacher, miracle worker and challenger to both institutions and individuals. And now she must stand and watch. On the other hand, Jesus acts despite his physical constraints. He cannot move. He is pinioned to the cross. He is exhausted, bleeding and filthy. Yet this is the man who extends the loving care of a mother to his mother. From his pain and his suffering, he commits his mother into the care of another man, one of his followers. And we are told, in that snippet of the gospel, that Jesus's wishes were respected. The Scriptures tell us that John found a place for Mary in his home.

From this point the passion is relentless torture for both man and mother. His weight gets heavier. His powers of recovery have long gone. His energy to sustain himself diminishes. The physical aspects of distress cannot be contained. They become vocal. There are various accounts of what was said by the dying Christ, but they mostly underpin this all too human aspect of the passion. It was painful. It was despairing. It was ugly.

In this place, where all gives out, where Jesus collapses on the cross, we are invited to join Mary as she gazes on the death of her son.

It was now about noon, and darkness came over the

whole land until three in the afternoon, while the sun's light failed; and the curtain of the temple was torn in two. Then Jesus, crying with a loud voice, said, 'Father, into your hands I commend my spirit.' Having said this, he breathed his last. (Luke 23.44–6)

In the arms of Mary

One of the most striking images of women on the way of the cross again involves the mother of Jesus. Yet again, we know this more by tradition than from scriptural sources. It is when the body of Jesus is taken down from the cross. We know this image very well. It has been caught in sculpture, painting and stained-glass window. We know the image as the *Pietà*. Mary, the mother, holds her dead son across her lap. It is a brutal parody of the nativity scenes likewise captured by innumerable artists. But this time the joy of birth is far from her.

For Christians there is the complex knowledge of many elemental and theological doctrines in gazing on this. Often the artist has captured the grief. We see the pain of the mother holding her dead son. Yet the reason it is such a powerful image for us is that the tragedy can be transcended. The *Pietà* cannot but capture the misery of death. A woman embraces the shell of her son's body. We know that the death that has led to this poignant moment is one that involves us. Indeed it is a death that is for us and that liberates us.

The *Pietà*, then, allows us to share in the passion of Jesus Christ on many levels. It presents us with the stark reminder that every death should provide us with: we too will die. None of us is immune. No one is excepted. Each and every one of us is going to die. However, through the offering of God through God in the death of Jesus, we are offered the hope of eternal life. Our sins fall from us in accepting the love of God epitomized in his death. So the *Pietà* image allows us to share in both the human and Godlike nature of the crucifixion.

The Orthodox fathers said of the incarnation that God became human so that humans could become Godlike. Or put another, probably better, way, the divine became human so the human could become divine. How does it achieve that? It does so through the crucifixion. In the crucifixion Jesus takes the sin of the world and transforms it.

There is, for all that, one very disconcerting factor involved in considering the *Pietà*: it is assumed. Like the meeting of Jesus and Mary on the way to Golgotha, it is pious tradition. The picture of Mary holding her dead son could almost be the image too far.

There is something of a tension in the stories of Jesus being laid in the tomb. It seems in some of the narratives that activity after Jesus's death is mainly confined to men. It is a man who asks for the release of the body of Jesus.

Now there was a good and righteous man named Joseph, who, though a member of the council, had not agreed to their plan and action. He came from the Jewish town of Arimathea, and he was waiting expectantly for the kingdom of God. This man went to Pilate and asked for the body of Jesus. Then he took it down, wrapped it in a linen cloth, and laid it in a rock-hewn tomb where no one had ever been laid. (Luke 23.50–3)

To accept that only men were involved would be erroneous. A Jew must be buried within a day of dying. And while Joseph of Arimathea is credited with gaining the body, there are discrepancies in the accounts of who prepared it for the tomb. In the Gospel of John it is another man, Nicodemus, who brings the spices. He carries out the task with Joseph. In the other three gospels these duties fall to women.

> The women who had come with him from Galilee followed, and they saw the tomb and how his body was laid. Then they returned and prepared spices and ointments. (Luke 23.56)

The gospel accounts give various names to the women who are involved in this. The mother of Jesus is not one of them. Where was Mary? We can only guess. Having walked the Via Dolorosa behind her son, having spoken with him as he hung nailed to the cross, having seen him die, we might well assume her to be in profound shock. Humans have the comfort and necessity of grief. It is for this reason that the *Pietà* becomes a touchstone for the human elements of the crucifixion. We know there is more to the crucifixion than human suffering. It is, after all, a co-mixture of the temporal and eternal. It is the place where the human and the godly meet in the same way as they meet in the resurrection.

Much is said in church rhetoric of the ordinariness of Mary. When we look at the span of her life we have to question that. Unique in witness, unique in her position, she is also alone in her grief. For that reason we celebrate her extraordinary qualities. These are apparent in the extreme in the passion. They make Mary a leading light among women on the way.

5

Mary Magdalene, apostle to the apostles

One woman stands out in any reading of the life, death and resurrection of Jesus Christ. That woman is mentioned a number of ways. She was healed by Jesus. She was a disciple of his. She heard him preach. She was a financial supporter of the retinue of Jesus. She saw him die. And she should be recognized as the first person to have seen him resurrected.

Mary Magdalene is perhaps the pre-eminent woman on the way. Her testimony has made her the apostle to the apostles. And yet this privileged position has, from time to time, been put at risk. The first person we considered in this book was the woman with the alabaster jar. As we saw in the Gospels of Matthew and Mark, the alabaster jar, which is traditionally associated with Mary Magdalene, is actually the property of another, unnamed woman. Yet many have not hesitated to turn her into Mary Magdalene.

Some of the most notable teachers of the Church have colluded in this misrepresentation. There have been times when they attempted to turn her into something she was not. They did this by clumsily putting together traditions and biblical stories that did not match. One instance of this was the seizing upon the sinful identity of the woman with the alabaster jar. It was taken one step further. Mary Magdalene somehow became a repentant whore. Unhindered by a lack of evidence she was turned into the woman taken in adultery. In transforming Mary Magdalene into a fallen woman the Church gave licence for all sorts of intellectual and artistic calumny.

By this process of myth-making she became a penitent after her forgiveness. This was a consequence of her realizing the enormity of her sinful past. She went into the wilderness where, along with personal vanity, she gave up wearing clothes. This provided patronized artists with an excuse to indulge in painting nudes or, at least, women in some stage of undress. The penitent Mary Magdalene gave a justification for titillation while seemingly adhering to strictures of only representing religious subjects. That the subject was without clothing was, of course, regrettable. But it was a necessary sacrifice in the name of improving art. After all, they were only portraying things 'as they were'.

Mary Magdalene was systematically marginalized. She was reduced to the subject of salacious entertainment. Mythology overtook scriptural information. Cult can supersede and pervert evidence. Much 'scholarship' was engaged in over the years to bend texts to suit the predilection of thinkers and writers. It was an easy next step to build on this misinformation.

How did all this occur? The reasons have to be guessed at. For some writers it may simply have been a case of a male-dominated Church wanting to do down the leading role of a strong woman. For others it was about demonology. It points to an unhealthy interest in the malady of one cured rather than the miraculous result. Illness is more interesting than health. Past takes precedence over the present.

The gospels do tell us that Mary Magdalene was healed by Jesus. This much we know. We are consistently told that seven demons were driven out of her. After that she became a key follower of Jesus as he went about in his active ministry. Scripture says she was one of those who maintained the coterie that followed Jesus.

Yet there is one facet that contends with the degradation of Mary Magdalene. She was the primary witness to an important consequence of the passion, the resurrection. She passed her testimony on to others. She is the model of mission for people of faith.

The Church claims that the death of Jesus has universal significance. It says that it is more than an historic event. Jesus Christ was crucified in Jerusalem. That is a fact. We do not have to rely just on the gospels for that information. Other sources confirm the trial, condemnation and execution of Jesus of Nazareth. Controversy starts after the death. What happens from then on is seen in a different light.

The development of the early Church, its spectacular success in gaining new members, has psychological, social and theological implications. People heard the good news and believed. They changed their lives. They were prepared to, and did, die for this faith. We are told that time and again in the book of the Acts of the Apostles. It is likewise recorded extensively in other historic sources. The deaths of believers served to help spread rather than quash the message of the Christ. These disciples spoke with their mouths and their lives. The claims about the death of Jesus and the implications of it – claims made then and still being made now – are an essential part of the faith. Letting others know of the benefits of the saviour's death is part of the ongoing task of those who follow the Christ.

The passion only makes sense in the context of the complete story. We have been looking at parts of a whole picture. By focusing on specific events on the way of the cross we have paused to consider snapshots on the way to something else. That is understandable. The passion fits into the life of the Christ. But there is a fuller reason hidden behind this partial methodology. The life of the Christ has power for believers because it has not ended. The power of the Christian message resides in a fuller story than a man stumbling on his way to execution.

And the Word became flesh and lived among us . . . (John 1.14)

That verse from the prologue to the Gospel of John is a touchstone of the Christian faith. Jesus was born. God became man. Yet that is not sufficient in itself. It is not the end of the story. The gospels go on to tell us of the teachings of Jesus. There are details of his travels. We witness some of the disturbances he created. We read of his recruitment of followers. Likewise we learn of his challenge to people to look at the way they live. We hear of the need for people to reassess their lives on a spiritual, personal and communal level. We follow his confrontation of the authorities. We are present at specific moments of change. He makes people whole. Jesus cures physical illness. He heals. He forgives sins.

This ministry has its apogee in the crucifixion. It is in the desolation of Golgotha that the Church proclaims the ongoing healing power of the Christ. The Christ forgave the sins of those who came into contact with him as he went about the Middle East of two thousand years ago. The Christ healed those who met him face to face. And the Church says that that forgiveness and healing is still available today. The life, death and resurrection of Jesus have meaning for people in the world here and now. We can still move to a place where we can be assured that our sins are forgiven. We, like those who saw Jesus in the flesh, can be made whole.

Just how this occurs is disputed. The polarities of traditional sacramental practice and biblical fundamentalism are just two manifestations of Christian belief. Between those poles there are many understandings and practices. For all that, the concept of forgiveness is central to the faith. How this is expressed is often more down to temperament tempered with church politics than anything else. What should unite the Christian Church is that the forgiveness of Jesus Christ can be reflected within the community of faith and the world at large.

A strengthening forgiveness

There is widespread acceptance and use within the Church of the sacrament of reconciliation. Sacramental confession and absolution allows people to confront their shortcomings, their sinfulness, and to receive the forgiveness of the Christ. This catholic understanding extends to the celebration of the eucharist. The Church celebrates the passion and all its benefits when it gathers for what is undoubtedly the central act of Christian worship. That is clear in what is said during eucharistic prayers throughout various denominations. Jesus becomes particularly present during the memorial recitation and celebration of what happened to him during his final hours on earth. By repetition we come closer to him. By reinforcement we are strengthened. The prayers are clear to state what good can and does flow from these events. This is to reinforce what the Church understands and proclaims in the passion and crucifixion.

The walk to the Place of the Skull liberates people. That is what the Church wants to share with those of little or no faith. It is a message it wants and needs to remind itself of again and again. Too often the Church can become absorbed in its own activity. Keeping the show on the road can take a lot of energy. But it is worth stepping back now and then and reminding ourselves that the Church has no power of its own. Any power the Church may have is that given to it by the Christ. Any influence it may use is a reflection of that power.

> . . . and we have seen his glory, the glory of a father's only son, full of grace and truth. (John 1.14)

The Church has a threefold task: to learn what it can about the liberating power of Jesus, to try to live within that freedom, and to pass on that message to others. This cannot be power for its own sake. It is an inverted power. Reward is promised but it is to be attained by surprising means.

> A dispute also arose among them as to which of them was to be regarded as the greatest. But he said to them, 'The kings of the Gentiles lord it over them; and those in authority over them are called benefactors. But not so with you; rather the greatest among you must become like the youngest, and the leader like one who serves. For who is greater, the one who sits at the table

or the one who serves? Is it not the one at the table? But I am among you as one who serves.' (Luke 22.24–7)

This inversion of status is exemplified by Jesus. Many of his followers deserted him because of it. The consequences of his teaching could seem extreme. But the Christ had told his followers that their discipleship could be painful. He warned them what to expect.

'I have told you these things to keep you from stumbling. They will put you out of the synagogues. Indeed, an hour is coming when those who kill you will think that by doing so they are offering worship to God.' (John 16.1–2)

We should not be surprised, then, at attempts to besmirch the reputations of Christians. We should be able to accept that people who have not encountered or comprehended the revolutionary message of faith in Jesus want to do down his followers. Yet it is with more than a modicum of disappointment and surprise that we realize such efforts were concentrated from within the Church on the apostle to the apostles, Mary Magdalene.

Detailed consideration of Mary Magdalene can only reassert her proper position. She is someone on whom we should rely. If there is a role model for an individual who has the truth in her grasp only to suffer at the hands of others – within and without the community of faith – it must be Mary Magdalene. She has been belittled. Her story has been corrupted. She was turned into a figure of salacious entertainment. And in every instance it serves, by design or otherwise, to betray her.

Mary Magdalene was given arguably the most important task of the gospel. She was the person to whom the resurrection was initially revealed. It is through Mary Magdalene that the Church received the message that Jesus lives. It is through this remarkable woman that the passion is confirmed as what the gospels show it to be, transfigured failure. The death of a criminal is overshadowed by the new life of the saviour.

How vital, then, it is that we should follow Mary Magdalene on the way of the cross. Her contacts with the suffering Jesus may have a poignancy with which we can transcend their tragic elements. That is because we are aware that her grief will be galvanized into joy. It is here we encounter our first difficulty. Mary Magdalene is mentioned only once during the passion. Indeed, before the events that lead up to the death of Jesus, she is mentioned on only one other occasion. That mention, however, is one that gives us an early indication of her importance. We learn that Mary Magdalene is one of those involved in the active support of the teaching ministry of Jesus.

> Soon afterwards he went on through cities and villages, proclaiming and bringing the good news of the kingdom of God. The twelve were with him, as well as some women who had been cured of evil spirits and infirmities: Mary, called Magdalene, from whom seven demons had gone out, and Joanna, the wife of Herod's steward Chuza, and Susanna, and many others, who provided for them out of their own resources. (Luke 8.1–3)

We have considered the role of these women in another chapter. What is important here is the qualified mention of Mary Magdalene. That she had been host to seven demons is a consistent piece of reportage. The fact is not alluded to until after the death of Jesus in the Gospel of

94

Mark. The author of John's Gospel mentions it when he tells us that Mary Magdalene stood at the foot of the cross with Jesus's mother and the disciple Jesus loved. In both cases the expulsion of demons is considered a matter worth noting. It makes her more specific. Mary Magdalene was not just any follower of Jesus. She is a follower with a past that connects her to him.

Many people had been cured and healed. Not all of them were made welcome by or considered necessary to the entourage of Jesus. In many cases he charged people not to let on how they came to be healed. This is a constant theme in the gospels. It is worth noting that the healings were not displays of disembodied magic. They consistently took place in the context of worship. Before curing a physical ailment, Jesus is often said to have prayed. Often he tells the person made whole that it is their faith that has brought about the miracle. At other times, after curing their illnesses, Jesus would urge people to go and give praise to God. By doing so, it would have to be assumed that the healed person would go and spread the message. There is an appealing contradiction in what he says to a man who is cured of leprosy.

A leper came to him begging him, and kneeling he said to him, 'If you choose, you can make me clean.' Moved with pity, Jesus stretched out his hand and touched him, and said to him, 'I do choose. Be made clean!' Immediately the leprosy left him, and he was made clean. After sternly warning him he sent him away at once, saying to him, 'See that you say nothing to anyone; but go, show yourself to the priest, and offer for your cleansing what Moses commanded, as a testimony to them.' (Mark 1.40–4)

It seems naive to ask the cured man to keep secret the source of the cure. It seems even more peculiar when, at the same time, he is commanded to declare publicly his cleanliness in front of a priest. If the man was known to suffer from the disease, it would be reasonable to expect people to be intrigued enough to ask how this cure came about. The gospel makes it clear that this dilemma was not faced. The man simply ignored Jesus's wishes.

> But he went out and began to proclaim it freely, so that Jesus could no longer go into a town openly, but stayed out in the country; and people came to him from every quarter. (Mark 1.45)

The contemporary interest in Jesus and his healings, and their subsequent proclamation in the gospels, makes the relative reticence on the casting out of seven demons from Mary Magdalene all the more intriguing. It is not unreasonable to think that there would be a detailed report of a woman who had undergone such a trauma only to become a major supporter of the apostles.

Stories of demons

It is not without precedent. The casting out of demons makes good copy for the authors of the gospels. What about the man with the unclean spirit who confronts Jesus when the disciples cross the sea to go into the country of the Gerasenes? He lives among the tombs, and we are told the man could not be contained, having broken his shackles and chains.

> When he saw Jesus from a distance, he ran and bowed down before him; and shouted at the top of his voice,

'What have you to do with me, Jesus, Son of the Most High God? I adjure you by God, do not torment me.' (Mark 5.6–7)

What follows is one of the most peculiar of all accounts in the gospels. Jesus rebukes the spirit and asks its name.

He replied, 'My name is Legion; for we are many.' (Mark 5.9)

At the request of the spirits, Jesus casts them out of the man and they take up residence in a nearby herd of swine. If that is not spectacular enough in itself, the spirits proceed to depart the scene in an astounding manner.

And the unclean spirits came out and entered the swine; and the herd, numbering about two thousand, rushed down the steep bank into the sea and were drowned in the sea. (Mark 5.13)

Much is then made of the man's recovery. He is of his right mind. He sits with Jesus and the disciples. The people who live in the region urge Jesus to leave their neighbourhood. They will tell the story. This tale is guaranteed more than local notoriety. The very recipient of Jesus's healing powers will be their broadcaster. He has a task other than to be a direct follower of Jesus.

As he was getting into the boat, the man who had been possessed by the demons begged that he might be with him. But Jesus refused, and said to him, 'Go home to your friends, and tell them how much the Lord has done for you, and what mercy he has shown you.' (Mark 5.19–20)

Little wonder that those who heard such reports were

97

amazed. Yet curiously, we are spared such intricacies when it comes to a woman who did become a key follower of Jesus and who provided for him and his entourage from her own means. The main reason must be that what she eventually became witness to was considered much more efficacious than the healing she herself received.

Mary Magdalene is the primary witness to the resurrection. But she is also a witness to the passion. She is mentioned before and after the death of Jesus. Unlike numerous other followers of Jesus, Mary Magdalene was at the scene of the crucifixion. And much is made of her noting that Jesus did die. For that reason her testimony is surer than many others'. She was there. Mary Magdalene was at the foot of the cross with the Blessed Virgin Mary and John.

At the foot of the cross

In the telling of this section of the passion, the author of John's Gospel sets a tableau that is famous in religious iconography. Jesus is on the cross on Golgotha and others look up to see him in his torment. This has been innumerably represented by painters. It is also the subject of much statuary, particularly in rood screens. The cross dominates a central part of the church, usually on a beam just in front of and above the sanctuary. In older churches this would have been on top of a screen. A number of ancient examples of these have survived protestant vandalism, notably in the West Country of England. The gothic revival movement of the nineteenth century made much use of screens and roods.

What is notable in such statuary is just who gets to be represented. And what is just as noteworthy, by corollary,

is who does not. The cross looms high. Jesus is nailed to it
and on either side, looking up in whatever attitude the
artist has chosen to represent – pain, grief, resolution,
desolation – are two figures. They are John and the mother
of Jesus. Mary Magdalene does not figure. She is depicted
in many paintings of the scene, which tend to have a wider
perspective, but she fails to enter the lists in rood screens.
What this sculptural representation is seeking to dramatize is the command of Jesus to the disciple he loved.

> When Jesus saw his mother and the disciple whom he
> loved standing beside her, he said to his mother,
> 'Woman, here is your son.' Then he said to the disciple,
> 'Here is your mother.' And from that hour the disciple
> took her into his own home. (John 19.26–7)

The very mention that Mary Magdalene was a witness
to this exchange in John's Gospel gives us room for
confidence that she also saw and heard what follows. She
hears Jesus say he is thirsty. She sees him offered sour wine
at the end of a branch of hyssop. She hears him speak.

> When Jesus had received the wine, he said, 'It is finished.'
> (John 19.30)

And she sees him die. She is like the author of John's
Gospel. Her testimony is not written. Yet it is still worth
noting.

> (He who saw this has testified so that you also may
> believe. His testimony is true, and he knows that he tells
> the truth.) (John 19.35)

This aspect of Mary Magdalene, that she was one of
those who saw him die, is what makes her evidence in
relation to the resurrection so vital. It is not just that Mary

Magdalene saw Jesus after his death. She saw him dead and laid in the grave. If one reads the various gospel accounts of the laying in the tomb, we come to realize that Mary Magdalene is one of a select number who are reported to have seen Jesus suffer on the cross, die and laid in the tomb.

When we read the gospels it is clear that her seeing Jesus dead is as important as her seeing him resurrected. Perhaps this is why in the synoptic gospels Mary Magdalene does not rate a mention until after the accounts of the death of Jesus are complete. There is substantial variation in these accounts, and because of that it is worth looking at each in some detail.

In Matthew, Mary Magdalene does not figure until after Jesus has cried out with a loud voice and breathed his last. The curtain of the temple has been torn in two. Tombs have opened and many of the saints have come back to life. The centurion declares that Jesus was truly God's son.

> Many women were also there, looking on from a distance . . . (Matthew 27.55)

In that very phrase their being 'also there' we have tacit augmentation of what the evangelist has told us. These women have watched the progression of events as he has outlined them. He then further vouches for their credibility. They are people of substance.

> . . . they had followed Jesus from Galilee and had provided for him. Among them were Mary Magdalene, and Mary the mother of James and Joseph, and the mother of the sons of Zebedee. (Matthew 27.55–56)

They are likewise mentioned as reliable witnesses to

the laying of the dead Jesus in the tomb of Joseph of Arimathea. They have seen the dead body of their teacher wrapped in a clean linen cloth. They have watched it placed in the new tomb hewn from rock after Joseph has gone to Pilate and asked for the body of his teacher. They remain after Joseph has rolled a great stone to seal the entrance to the grave.

Mary Magdalene and the other Mary were there, sitting opposite the tomb. (Matthew 27.61)

This is confirmed, albeit with different components, in the order of events given by the writers of the gospels of both Mark and Luke. Mark's account differs in naming those who accompanied Mary Magdalene. It says Mary, the mother of James the younger and Joses, and Salome were with her. But it agrees with Matthew's version of Joseph of Arimathea going, boldly this time, to Pilate to ask for the body of Jesus, of wrapping it in a linen cloth and rolling a stone across the entrance to the tomb.

Mary Magdalene and Mary the mother of Joses saw where the body was laid. (Mark 15.47)

We infer Mary Magdalene's presence in Luke. She will be named later as passing on the news of the resurrection to the disciples. Up until then it is only 'women who had followed him from Galilee' who are mentioned. If this assumption is correct, then we can confirm what has been said in Matthew and Mark. Joseph secures the dead body of Jesus.

The women who had come with him from Galilee followed, and they saw the tomb and how his body was laid. (Luke 23.55)

The empty tomb

All this detail has a purpose. Each of the writers of the life and death of Jesus is pointing to yet another, more important, event. And it is in that event that Mary Magdalene features so prominently. In Matthew, Mary Magdalene, along with the others, goes to the tomb. There is an earthquake. An angel comes and rolls back the stone from the entrance to the tomb. The angel gives them the message to tell the disciples. On their way, they meet the resurrected Christ.

> And they came to him, took hold of his feet, and worshipped him. Then Jesus said to them, 'Do not be afraid; go and tell my brothers to go to Galilee; there they will see me.' (Matthew 28.10)

In Mark's Gospel the stone has already been moved out of the way. A young man dressed in white is sitting there and commissions them to tell Peter and the disciples. This time they are struck with fear and say nothing to anyone. In the longer ending of this gospel, Mary Magdalene is especially blessed.

> Now after he rose early on the first day of the week, he appeared first to Mary Magdalene, from whom he had cast out seven demons. She went out and told those who had been with him, while they were mourning and weeping. (Mark 16.9–10)

In Luke's Gospel there are two men dressed in dazzling white clothes. They confront the women with a new reality after posing an astonishing question.

> The women were terrified and bowed their faces to the ground, but the men said to them, 'Why do you look for

the living among the dead? He is not here, but has risen.' (Luke 24.5)

For all these variations, there is one message. The Jesus they followed, watched die on the cross, saw dead in the tomb, is alive. This is powerful stuff. One might expect a rapturous reception to such glad tidings. The response is startling. The disciples simply refuse to believe Mary Magdalene and the other women. Perhaps this is the root cause of the belittling of Mary Magdalene in subsequent ages. The women have had this experience because they have dared to go to the tomb. We can only guess at their motives – duty, love or some other reason. But by doing so they have left the other disciples to their own timidity. It is understandable that they were sad and confused. Yet into their despondency comes wonderful news. It comes out of the mouths of women. They tell the others that they have seen that the dead Jesus is raised. And those who were the front-line followers of Jesus refuse to believe them. Mary Magdalene is distrusted.

How poignant then becomes the telling of the resurrection appearance in John. Mary Magdalene comes to the tomb on her own. She sees that the stone at the entrance has been moved, so goes to get Simon Peter and 'the other disciple', John. The writer makes much of who got there first, who entered and who first believed. Their profession of faith is impeccable. After that, the disciples leave. A solitary figure is left in the garden.

But Mary stood weeping outside the tomb. As she wept, she bent over to look into the tomb; and she saw two angels in white, sitting where the body of Jesus had been lying, one at the head and the other at the feet. (John 20.11–12)

The angels ask Mary Magdalene the cause of her grief. She is distressed, she says, because the body of Jesus has been taken away. We do not know who she thinks is responsible for this. She says simply that 'they' have taken the body. Then something happens to dispel her grief and dismay.

> When she had said this, she turned around and saw Jesus standing there, but she did not know it was Jesus. Jesus said to her, 'Woman, why are you weeping?' (John 20.14–15)

This is the same question put to her by the angels. But Jesus asks a further question. He wants to know who she is looking for. Mary Magdalene pleads for the body of her teacher.

> Supposing him to be the gardener, she said to him, 'Sir, if you have carried him away, tell me where you have laid him, and I will take him away. Jesus said to her, 'Mary!' (John 20.15–16)

Touch me not

Much has rightly been made of this. Jesus calls Mary by her name. It is his calling of her, person to person, that allows her to recognize the Christ. Up to this point she does not know who he is. She has assumed him to be someone else. But when he says her name, she sees. She then addresses him.

> She turned and said to him in Hebrew, 'Rabbouni!' (which means Teacher). (John 20.16)

This scene has been the subject of many paintings. The worshipping disciple is on her knees in front of a young man, usually draped in a loosened shroud. He has been wounded. The marks of the nails in his hands and feet are clear. But there is no doubt that he is alive. While this fills her with joy, Jesus impresses upon her the need to share this news. It is not something to be held exclusively.

Jesus said to her, 'Do not hold on to me, because I have not yet ascended to the Father. But go to my brothers and say to them, "I am ascending to my Father and your Father, to my God and your God."' Mary Magdalene went and announced to the disciples, 'I have seen the Lord'; and she told them that he had said these things to her. (John 20.18)

John's Gospel gives the vignette that has become the study for countless works of art. A woman sees the saviour and reaches towards him. She does not touch him. She cannot. The paintings are often called *Noli me tangere* – do not touch me. But John's Gospel gives something more astonishing. This account is followed by belief. The disciples do not choose to disbelieve this woman. They do not discount what she says. Mary Magdalene's testimony is accepted for what it is. She is the person who first saw Jesus alive again. By believing what she tells them, they accord her a great honour. This honour affirms Mary Magdalene in her rightful place. She is the apostle of the resurrection. She is the one who has given us the news, which we are charged to pass on. Jesus Christ was born, died, and is risen. Alleluia!

Moreover, some women of our group astounded us

The writing of this book has been carried out with an awareness of a number of contradictions. One is clearly displayed on the cover. It is a contradiction seen by looking at the title and the name of the author. It resides in the simple fact that there is a biological shortfall between the subject and the writer. The book's title takes as its starting point women. I am a man. For a man to presume to be able to give any detailed reflection on the passion of the Christ from a feminine angle has to be just that, presumption. Yet there is little I can do about this aspect of who I am. Gender is a given. And the topic I have sought to address cannot be changed. It is a path within the shadow of a realization of that conundrum that I have presumed to walk.

For all that, it is proper that I attempt to walk it. Firstly, it undergirds the stated methods of the book: to set out on the way, not directly relying on external sources, but using the gifts of imagination; to use an individual or a group captured in Scripture and tradition and see where they may lead us. This has inevitably been something of a crooked path. The mind does not always stay as focused as we might hope. Meditation can have a life of its own. Thoughts wander. We follow their movement.

Yet there is an impetus within this. It has a dynamic that can and should propel us. The story of the passion of the Christ has power because of something beyond it. The nadir of the sufferings of Jesus has a counterbalance. The zenith is in the resurrection. The pains leading up to his crucifixion and in his death are made whole in the victory over death. We can move through consideration of his suffering and anguish, knowing there will be a joyful resolution to them.

This is borne out by some of the women on the way. They were immediate witnesses to pain. Yet they were transformed into messengers of joy. As we saw with Mary Magdalene, not everyone was receptive to this. The disciples were almost overwhelmed by the death of Jesus. They had withdrawn into a private world. But the public key had been revealed to women who could testify to the empty tomb and more. These initially personal experiences impelled them to give out the news that the Christ had not been vanquished by death. They had to share the good news.

This, again, is a point of contradiction. The grieving and fearful band of followers of Jesus were closed in on their own feelings. They had been overtaken by malaise. At first they could not take in the importance of what the women were telling them. They could not grasp that Jesus is alive.

Now it was Mary Magdalene, Joanna, Mary the mother of James, and the other women with them who told this to the apostles. But the words seemed to them an idle tale, and they did not believe them. (Luke 24.10–11)

108

The disciples' timidity was broken through by the Christ. In his revelation to the first witnesses, Jesus gave power and purpose to the Church to transcend the doom and gloom. He could show them the way forward. In John's Gospel a personal revelation to Mary Magdalene became a message to the disciples and, by corollary, to the world. The singular message of that precise time became one with a universal and timeless impact.

An isolated incident had rich rewards. Those benefits have not been exhausted. This dichotomy between the individual and the broader community continues today. What holds true for an individual may be of some validity to others. This tension between the individual and the corporate is a creative one. For the Church it is more than creative. It is essential. No personal experience can be fenced off. The personal should feed into the wider life of the believing community.

The story continues

The gospels are part of our resources for the ongoing telling of the Christian story. Yet as we can see in the post-resurrection stories, they can show elements of tension between one person's experience and a community's refusal to acknowledge that experience. The gospels do not always agree. One gospel may have accounts of an event that does not appear in another. The evangelist's aim was to let others know what he, or the people he was with, had come to learn about Jesus. The writers drew together a range of stories to make sure they were not forgotten. Each did so with a target audience in mind. Yet their efforts have far exceeded their initial goals. The gospel accounts have come to have a life of their own. And that life is absorbed in the lives of individuals. It is reflected in the ongoing corporate life of the Church.

The authors of the four gospels give us a literary start on the challenge of Christian living. One should not presume to pronounce on its ending. That is because there can be no one ending here. It is, more importantly, a common ending. The real ending is in God. Until we reach that end we have a task. That is to let others know what Mary Magdalene and the women knew. We should be telling people these stories.

In doing so, we return to the tension between the individual and the corporate. Many people were involved in a joint venture, which was the proclamation of Jesus as the Christ. Many people are still engaged in that venture. The Church is the coming together of many people's stories. Its task is to bring them together under God in the Christ. Having brought them together, it makes them public. Its method is the proclamation of Jesus in the lives of people today, while respecting and recounting the writings, traditions and gifts of former times. It is far more than a personally appropriated apprehension of God.

Nor can the passion of Jesus Christ be reduced to some kind of a generalized feeling of discomfort with the pain and anguish of existence. The story of the Christ's suffering is much more than that. It is more than an account of one man's pain. It is also a challenge. This takes us beyond mere navel-gazing. A person with faith is not only engaged in the business of an ongoing working out of a personal plan to accept God's gift in Jesus. Such an individual struggle must also have a social dimension to it. A Christian has a personal faith that insists on membership of something larger. Membership of the Church means there is a group acceptance of God's gift of freedom, which is revealed to us in the death and resurrection of Jesus Christ. This again has a further social dimension to it. The Church must be involved in the world outside its own boundaries. There is a commission that comes with faith.

> Then he opened their minds to understand the scriptures, and he said to them, 'Thus it is written, that the Messiah is to suffer and to rise from the dead on the third day, and that repentance and forgiveness of sins is to be proclaimed to all nations, beginning from Jerusalem.' (Luke 24.45–7)

To reduce the salvation of the world, the actions of the Christ on the cross, to some claim of private ownership is dangerous. It is more than that. It is obscene. In looking at the passion of Jesus Christ we look at a public event with universal implications. The privatization of our age extends to matters spiritual. We see it in church and personal spirituality. This has to be opposed. We must economize our energies in this field. We have to draw people together. We must resist the movement to privatize salvation.

For all that, we still need an individual way into the Christian story. Looking at particular incidents in the passion has given us an entry point into a universal message. It has been a technique to bring us face to face with the Christ. Not to use such an entrée runs the risk of ineptitude. We have good cause to shrink from the task. The whole experience could be too much. It can overpower us. This can only happen if we think our personal entry is isolated from others'. So we include ourselves particularly within the number of others who have perceived or are trying to come to terms with the universal action of the Christ.

111

In our tracing of the passion we have drawn on both scriptural and apocryphal sources. There has been a particular springboard for this. We have looked at one group of people, the women in the passion. By looking to them we have seen how they have been regarded and treated. Some of these women have been misunderstood. Others have been the victims of the working out of others' fears. And, it has to be admitted, some have been the victims in the exercise of some men's fantasies. Some have had their reputations tarnished because they were considered too powerful. They were too strong a pointer to Jesus Christ and his actions. Some, we have had to accept in all honesty, may not have existed.

There is a unifying quality to the stories of the women, whatever the embellishments, compromises or detractions that have been made upon, with or to them. These women have led and still lead us beyond themselves. Their individual contacts can have a wider impact. This is not only for our individual benefit. Something greater is involved. They point beyond humanity. They lead inevitably to God. The women do not do this of their own volition. They do it through contact. They do it through their contacts with Jesus. It is thanks to them and through them that we may have some deeper insight into what the passion means. We may begin to see it with new eyes.

It is the women's purpose to display the duality of human existence. Firstly, there is a singular event. There is a particular contact with the suffering Jesus as he makes his way to death on the cross. But there is also a wider spin-off. What involves each of them has implications beyond the individual. It has universal significance. It includes each and every one of us. Thereby their contacts with the tortured Christ come to have a corporate dimension. They

112

contain effects the women themselves could not have guessed at.

Each person, woman or man, who came into contact with Jesus was on the verge of a potentially life-changing event. The irony is that they may not have appreciated this. For them it was an event that may or may not have added significance. We have the gift of distance to see what they gained. We can see what they benefited from. And we have an added luxury. We can see the inverse. We can see what, on occasion, they missed. We know what they failed to embrace for their own betterment. Some people, like the early disciples, immediately accepted the call to follow. Others flirted with the idea. Still others tried it out for a while and fell by the wayside. Some found the demands too difficult. The teaching was too uncomfortable. They found themselves in the society of others they would prefer not to mix with. The whole experience was too draining. They wanted succour. They were given discomfort. Whatever the reason, they did not stick with it.

However, if we are to hope to draw anything from these women on the way, it must be cast in more than retrospective reflection. There should be a contemporary impact. Their connections with the Christ spill over to us and to where we find ourselves today. The gospels should not be remote. For people of faith they have immediate power. The stories of Jesus are more than mere records of events. Indeed, they cannot be used as mere registers of history. They transcend what they contain. They must have a future. They do. By meditating and musing on the incidents the gospels contain, we are dealing with a challenge for today. The challenge, as it is often put simply and confusingly, is this: to become more Christlike.

If one sets the goal to become more Christlike then one

113

has to extend oneself well beyond the sphere of private understanding and piety. The Christian gospel is both a personal and corporate gospel. It is not one at the expense of the other. It is always holding the two in tension. What an individual does is done in relation to other individuals and groups. No one is alone.

> For just as the body is one and has many members, and all the members of the body, though many, are one body, so it is with Christ. For in the one Spirit we were all baptized into one body – Jews or Greeks, slave or free – and we were all made to drink of one Spirit. (1 Corinthians 12.12–13)

One way to remind us of that is by recognizing gender. The stories of the women in the passion continue in the body of the Church. Recalling them has not been an end in itself. The process has not been to lead us to a terminus. Their stories have allowed us to look both back to and beyond the passion. We have recollected and meditated on other people mentioned in the gospel stories. We have revisited healings in the breadth of Jesus's ministry. He made people whole, be it physically, mentally or spiritually.

The challenge of Jesus

Through this, along with the teachings of the Christ, we have attempted to focus our attention on the person of Jesus. We have seen his acceptance of people. We have witnessed the open-mindedness of Jesus. We have heard his challenge. We have been confronted by his anger. We may have been unnerved by his disturbance of the socially accepted mores. We have looked to the Christ and we have felt looked on by him.

This, I hope, has been more than a mere academic exercise. We may have learned more about certain aspects of tradition, story and Scripture on the way. We may have encountered aspects of the Christian treasury we do not approve of. That cannot be a bad thing. It adds to the collective memory that is part of the riches of the Church. But the aim has been to look at incidents in a discursive way. That is reflective of the way many of us think. We do not all take an idea and systematically and doggedly work it through. Some of us do. But not all of us can.

The process in this book has not been to look at ideas alone. It has sought to visit incidents. These incidents focus on the interaction of persons. In these exchanges one person is the constant. It is Jesus. This is consonant with our faith. A Christian is always trying to encounter Jesus. This can be through one of a wide range of methods. It can be through prayer. It can be through meditation. Or it can be through experience.

For instance, if we want to understand the Christian insight into caring for the ill, we can do worse than think of Veronica. When we wash the face of an injured person, we can be as Veronica. We can be washing the face of Jesus. A person who is accepting such a ministry has the frightening privilege of representing the Christ. They need not be aware of this. But accepting assistance is a Christlike action. Looking at a person offering us help in our need allows us to look through God's eyes. When someone renders us assistance, we can fruitfully recall that Jesus accepted assistance from Veronica. This imaginative exercise allows us to see ourselves in a rounder, fuller way.

This is, of course, presumption. I have already admitted the presumptuous nature of this entire project. We must check that presumption is not a prelude to arrogance. We

115

cannot be Jesus. We cannot be God. These are merely imaginative keys to assist us in deepening our understanding of God in Jesus in the passion. And by looking at the women on the way we see an interaction.

A recurring technique of this book has been to move in and out of the passion. We have gone forward and back from events recorded in Scripture. We have diverted from narrative or pious tradition. This is right and proper. We know the story of the birth, life, death and resurrection of Jesus. That is the wholeness we seek to draw on. It is not wholeness just for ourselves. It has a completeness way beyond that. Its completeness resides in the existence of God. It is before the world, in the world, and of the world to come. By the birth of Jesus we have a locus in history. God became human at a definite time. It occurred in a specific place. From that time and place we see the history of the world differently. We look to the time before the birth of the Christ in a revised way.

Yet for many people an encounter with the Christ is beyond history. There is no point at very first contact with someone who knows little or nothing about Jesus in merely suggesting that they read the Bible. That may be useful in some cases. It may be helpful for some in the future. The keyhole to Christian living is the person to whom the declaration of ignorance is being made. If someone says they know nothing about God we have to lead them to a point where they might see that they are wrong. It could be that they do have such knowledge. Or if we have a particular teaching bent, we could let them know that there are people around them who think they know more about it than the person making the admission. Contact between them may lead them to exploring new avenues of thought.

I am aware that again it makes what we have been doing

116

for the most part cerebral. But I am actually trying to warn against that. It is up to us to use the brain for a social purpose. The privatization of faith is often linked to an over-intelligent embracing of the salvation story. The story of the life of Jesus should not be restricted to a simple, repeatable template of encounter, realization of personal sinfulness and conversion. To do so diminishes the reality of the Christ's liberation.

Reading the gospels is a humbling experience. What we see Jesus display is a flexibility that can only be wondered at. Jesus meets the individual precisely. There is no general response in him or to him. The individual matters. The buzz language of the moment is that Jesus meets people where they are. If a person is a sinner, he forgives them. If they have faith, he rewards it. If they need solace, he gives it. If they require a mental kick up the backside, the foot of Jesus is ready to do the job. He challenges where challenge is needed. He rebukes where necessary. He comforts. He heals. He makes whole.

The thing to be wondered at is not that there is a general experience of Jesus, but that the experience of Jesus is unique to each person. It is in that specificity that the modern age runs the risk of losing the plot. Because it is a unique encounter – Jesus meets the very person in front of him – many try to appropriate the Christ for purely personal use. The personal can only make sense when it is linked to the communal. That is what a community of faith, a church, is for. It is not there solely to validate personal experiences. It is there to underpin the universal quality to the mission and ministry of Jesus.

We can see this through the women in the passion. The woman with the alabaster jar, Veronica, the women of Jerusalem, the Blessed Virgin Mary and Mary Magdalene bring us into contact with Jesus. Those contacts are intense and profound. But they are also continuing. That is the gospel element of these contacts with Jesus. What the women saw, said and did had power. It had power for the women involved. And it still has power. It is powerful for us today. We gain that power through meditation and reflection on their contacts with Jesus. We cannot appropriate it. We may approximate it.

This is especially borne out through the post-resurrection appearances. The women who astounded the apostles had a real experience with Jesus. They were empowered to spread the message. We have seen how Mary Magdalene is the sole consistent primary witness to the resurrection. She, alone with the other women mentioned in various accounts, saw the risen Christ. But the importance of this witness lay in the consequences. These women were not timid. They may have been frightened. Yet they had a greater task. Their function was to spread the astounding news. It was astounding for them personally. And it was astonishing for the followers of the Christ. It was for the individual and for the broader community of the church. Their apprehension of the new risen reality was confronting. This is clearly stated by two disciples when they tell the man they have not yet recognized as Jesus:

> 'Moreover, some women of our group astounded us. They were at the tomb early this morning, and when they did not find his body there, they came back and told us that they had indeed seen a vision of angels who said that he was alive. Some of those who were with us went to the tomb and found it just as the women had said; but they did not see him.' (Luke 24.22–4)

Sophia – the name of Wisdom

Knowledge of this post-resurrection Jesus inflamed the Church. It inspired people to regain their faith in their teacher. It empowered them to go to death and beyond. The same knowledge is at work in the world today. It challenges both the inner and outer lives of those coming to terms with their faith. It brings into question the personal and the social behaviour of those who call themselves Christian. No part of life is exempted from it. It is wisdom. Wisdom, in the Bible, is depicted as female. Its nature is captured in its very name, Sophia.

The women on the way astound us because they do not hold on to their experiences. By reading and meditating on them today we can become involved and we can then go on to share the experience. In this way we share Sophia, wisdom. Wisdom cannot be held back. It has an imperative social dimension.

'Come to me, you who desire me,
and eat your fill of my fruits.
For the memory of me is sweeter than honey,
and the possession of me sweeter than the
    honeycomb.
Those who eat of me will hunger for more,
and those who drink of me will thirst for more.
Whoever obeys me will not be put to shame,
and those who work with me will not sin.'

All this is the book of the covenant of the
    Most High God,
the law that Moses commanded us
as an inheritance for the congregations of Jacob.

It overflows like the Pishon, with wisdom,
and like the Tigris at the time of the first fruits.
It runs over, like the Euphrates, with
    understanding,
and like the Jordan at harvest time.
It pours forth instruction like the Nile,
like the Gihon at the time of vintage.
The first man did not know wisdom fully,
nor will the last one fathom her.
For her thoughts are more abundant than the sea,
and her counsel deeper than the great abyss.

As for me, I was like a canal from a river,
like a water channel into a garden.
I said, 'I will water my garden
and drench my flower beds.'
And lo, my canal became a river,
and my river a sea.
I will again make instruction shine forth like
    the dawn,
and I will make it clear from far away.
I will again pour out teaching like prophecy,
and leave it all to future generations.
Observe that I have not laboured for myself alone,
but for all who seek wisdom.
(Ecclesiasticus 24.19–34)